Code Of Canon Law

Canon 66 «The Christian economy, therefore, since it is the new and definitive Covenant, will never pass away; and no new public revelation is to be expected before the glorious manifestation of our Lord Jesus Christ." Yet even if Revelation is already complete, it has not been made completely explicit; it remains for Christian faith gradually to grasp its full significance over the course of the centuries.

Canon 67 Throughout the ages, there have been so-called «private» revelations, some of which have been recognized by the authority of the Church. They do not belong, however, to the deposit of faith. It is not their role to improve or complete Christ's definitive Revelation, but to help live more fully by it in a certain period of history. Guided by the Magisterium of the Church, the sensus fidelium knows how to discern and welcome in these revelations whatever constitutes an authentic call of Christ or his saints to the Church.

Christian faith cannot accept "revelations" that claim to surpass or correct the Revelation of which Christ is the fulfilment, as is the case in certain non-Christian religions and also in certain recent sects which base themselves on such "revelations."

The Full of Grace:
The Early Years.
The Merit.
Joseph's Passion.
The Blue Angel.
The Boyhood of Jesus.

Follow Me:
Treasure with 7 Names
Where there are Thorns, there also will be roses
For Love that Perseveres
The Apostolic College
The Decalogue

The Chronicles of Jesus & Judas Iscariot:
I See You As You Are
Those who are Marked
Jesus Weeps

Lazarus:
That Beautiful Blonde
Flowers of Bounty

Claudia Procula:
Do You Love the Nazarene?
The Caprice of Court Morals

Christian Tenets:
On Reincarnation

Mary of Magdala:
Ah! My Beloved! I Reached You At Last!

Lamb Books
Illustrated adaptations for the whole family

LAMB BOOKS

Published by Lamb Books, 2 Dalkeith Court, 45 Vincent Street, London SW1P
4HH;
UK, USA, FR, IT, SP, PT, DE

www.lambbooks.org

First published by Lamb Books 2013
This edition
001
Text copyright @ Lamb Books Nominee, 2013
Illustrations copyright @ Lamb Books, 2013
The moral right of the author and illustrator has been asserted
All rights reserved

The author and publisher are grateful to the Centro Editoriale Valtoriano in Italy
for Permission to quote from the Poem of the Man- God by Maria Valtorta, by
Valtorta Publishing

Set in Palatino Linotype R
Printed and bound by CPI Group (UK) Ltd, Croydon, CR0, 4YY
Except in the USA, this book is sold subject to the condition that it shall not,
by way of trade or otherwise, be lent, resold, hired out, or otherwise circulated
without the publisher's prior consent in any form of binding or cover other than
that in which it is published and without a similar condition including this
condition being imposed on the subsequent purchaser

Follow Me

Where There Are **Thorns**,
There **&**lso Will Be **Roses**

LAMBBOOKS

Acknowledgements

The material in this book is adapted from 'The Poem of the Man+God' (The Gospel As Revealed To Me) by Maria Valtorta, first approved by Pope Pius XII in 1948, when, in a meeting on February 26th 1948, witnessed by three other priests, he ordered the three priest present to "Publish this work as it is".
In 1994, the Vatican heeded to the calls of Christians worldwide and have begun to examine the case for the Canonization of Maria Valtorta (Little John).

The Poem of the Man God was described by Pope Pius' confessor as "edifying". Mystical revelations have long been the province of priests and the religious. Now, they are accessible to all. May all who read this adaptation, also find it edifying. And through this light, may Faith be renewed. Special Thanks to the Centro Editoriale Valtortiano in Italy for permission to quote from the Poem of the Man God by Maria Valtorta, nick named, Little John.

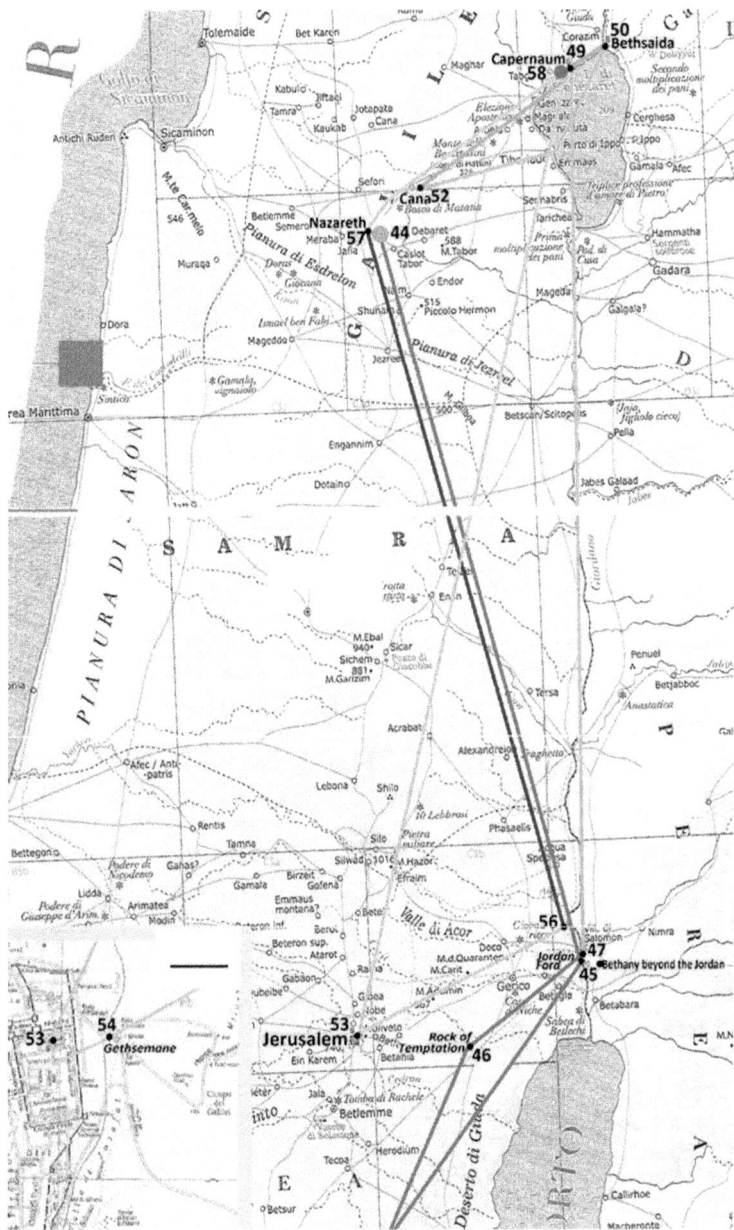

Contents

Jesus At The Wedding At Cana.

The wedding venue is a long low white house in the outskirts of Cana, set in the middle of a grassy open space with some fig and apple trees and a well at its centre. It is owned by farmers who live in the middle of their holding, surrounded by calm green country that stretches far beyond it. The house faces the road but is set a little way off what looks like a main road to which it is linked by a path that runs through the grassy ground. On the ground level of the house, a few low doors, not more than two on each side, open into low dark rooms where the family actually lives, where they have their store-room and wine cellar.

An outside staircase along the front climbs up to the door of the first floor situated about half way up the facade and leads into a hall used for special occasions like feast days or for tasks that require a lot of space like drying and pressing foodstuffs. There are a few windows and doors, and a terraced roof surrounded by a low wall of about a metre high. A shady vine pergola reaches up to the sunny terrace, stretching its branches over more than half of it.

It is not yet nine o'clock in the morning in springtime. The corn in the fields is still young and green and

earless. The meadows are covered in grass and the dew
on the grass makes the country look greener. The leaves
of the fig tree and the apple-tree are green and tender as
are those of the vines. But there are neither flowers nor
fruits on the apple-tree, the fig-tree nor on the vines, the
apple tree only having recently shed its blooms and its
little fruit not yet visible.

It is a bright and sunny day; the air is still free from dust
and the sky is completely blue. There is complete calm
without movement or sound. And then two women in
long dresses and wearing mantles that cover also their
heads like veils, emerge on the main road and then turn
into the path that leads up to the house.

The older of the two women, about fifty years old, is
wearing a dark dress made from raw wool of a greyish
brown hue.
The younger woman is dressed in a pale yellow dress and
a blue mantle, looks about 35 years old, is startlingly
beautiful and slender and carries Herself with much
dignity perfumed with much kindness and humility. As
She draws nearer, Her pale face, blue eyes and blond hair
visible on Her forehead identify Her to be our Most Holy
Lady but the older woman remains unknown.

The two women are conversing and Mary is smiling.
When they are nearer to house, someone who has
obviously been watching their arrival, informs the others
in the house and two men and two women, all in their
best clothes, go out to meet them and give the arriving
guest a most hearty welcome.

Mary, Who is either a relative or a close friend of the
bridegroom's family and therefore on familiar terms with
them, is most warmly welcomed and then escorted by an
elderly man, the landlord, up the outside staircase and

into a large hall that seems to occupy most, if not all of the upstairs space. It has been cleared of every object and then decorated with branches, mats and tables set with rich dishes. There are two tables laid out for guests; one at the centre and another along the right hand wall. The table at the centre is richly laid, with amphorae and plates full of fruit. The one along the right wall is not quite as sumptuously prepared as the table at the centre. There is also a long dresser against the left wall that is laid out with plates of cheese, honey covered cakes and sweetmeats whilst on the floor, beneath the dresser, there are more amphorae and also six large vases shaped like copper jars.

Mary, listens benignly to what they tell Her and then She takes off Her mantle and kindly helps to finish laying the tables; going to and fro sorting out the bed-seats, straightening up wreaths of flowers, improving the appearance of the fruit dishes, making sure that the lamps are filled with oil, all the while smiling, speaking very little and when She does, in a very low voice. But She listens a great deal and with much patience.

A loud sound of musical instruments not very harmonious wafts into the hall from the road and with the exception of Mary, they all rush out, led by the groom, to welcome the bride, who comes in, walking by his side, smartly dressed and happy and surrounded by friends and relatives.

Meanwhile, Jesus, in a white tunic and a dark blue mantle, has arrived at the village together with John and Judas Thaddeus. When Judas hears the sound of instruments, he questions a man nearby and then speaks with Jesus, Who smiles and says 'Let us go and make My Mother happy.'
And they start walking across the fields towards the

house. Jesus' arrival is observed by the same watchman
as before, who then informs the others. The landlord,
with his son the bridegroom and Mary, all go down to
meet Him and greet Him respectfully and also His
companions.
The loving and respectful manner in which Jesus and
Mary greet each other is particularly touching; there are
no effusions as they exchange the words 'Peace be with
You' each with a look and a smile worth a hundred
embraces and a hundred kisses. A kiss trembles on
Mary's lips but is not given. Instead, She lays Her little
white hand on Jesus' Shoulder and lightly touches a curl
of His long hair; the caress of a chaste lover.

Then, walking by His Mother, Jesus climbs up the
staircase, followed by His disciples, the landlord and then
the groom. As they enter the hall, the women begin to
bustle about, adding seats and plates to the table at the
centre for the three unexpected guests; Jesus' coming
having been uncertain and that of His companions
completely unforeseen.

'May peace be in this house and the blessing of God on
you all' says Jesus in His distinct sweet, full virile, voice
as He enters the hall majestically, dominating all present
with His bearing and His height. Though a casual guest,
He seems more the king of the banquet than the groom
or the landlord, regardless of how humble and obliging
He is. The two disciples are also invited to sit at the same
table out of respect for Jesus.

Jesus takes His place at the table next to the Landlord,
sitting directly across from Mary, Who's place is by the
bride. The mothers of the young couple are also seated at
this table but all the other women are seated at the other
table by the right wall where they are making a din worth
of a hundred people.

Jesus sits with His back turned to the wall where the dresser and large jars are so He cannot see them. Nor can He see the steward bustling about the dishes of roast meat which are brought in for the guests via a door by the dresser. The young couple and the guests of importance are served first and then followed by the table at the right.

The banquet begins and the guests lack neither appetite nor thirst except for Jesus and His Mother Who both eat and drink little. Mary speaks very little. Jesus talks a little more but although very moderate, He is neither sullen nor disdainful in the little He says. He is kind but not talkative; He answers when He is questioned, responds when spoken to, takes an interest in the subject and states His opinion but then He concentrates on His thoughts as one accustomed to meditation. He smiles but He never laughs and if He hears an inconsiderate joke, He pretends He has not heard. Mary is nourished by the contemplation of Her Jesus, and so is John, who is at the end of the table and hangs on His Master's lips.

Mary notices that the servants are talking in low voices to the steward, who looks very embarrassed and She understands what the cause of the unpleasant situation is. 'Son ', She whispers in a low voice, thus drawing Jesus' attention.

'Son, they have no more wine.'

'Woman, what is there still between Me and You?' Jesus says, smiling at Her even more gently, and Mary smiles back like two people aware of some truth which is their joyful secret but is ignored by everyone else.

In that smile, Jesus says to His Mother, without words: "Before I was Yours, only Yours. You gave Me orders, and I obeyed You. I was subject to You. Now I belong to My mission."

And in that one word "still" He says: "You were
everything for Me, Mother, as long as I was only Jesus of
Mary of Nazareth, and You are everything in My spirit;
but since I became the expected Messiah, I belong to My
Father. Wait for a little while and once My mission is over,
I will be, once again, entirely Yours; You will hold Me
once again in Your arms, as when I was a little child, and
no one will ever again contend with You for Your Son,
considered as the disgrace of mankind, who will throw
His mortal remains at You, to bring on You the shame of
being the mother of a criminal. And afterwards You will
have Me once again, triumphant, and finally You will
have Me forever when You are triumphant in Heaven. But
now I belong to all these men. And I belong to the Father,
Who sent Me to them."

'Do what He will tell you.' Mary says to the servants. In
the smiling eyes of Her Son, Mary has read His consent,
veiled by the great teaching to all those "who are called".
'Fill the jars with water ' says Jesus to the servants.
The servants go out to the well, the pulleys screech as
the dripping pail is lowered, pulled up and lowered again
and the jars are filled with water brought from the well.

The steward pours out some of the liquid with astonished
eyes, then tastes it with gestures of even greater
astonishment, relishes it and then speaks to the landlord
and the groom.
Mary looks at Her Son once again, and smiles; then
having received a smile from Him, She bows Her head,
blushing slightly. She is happy.
A murmur spreads throughout the hall, they all turn
their heads towards Jesus and Mary, some stand up to
get a better view, some go near the jars. Then a moment's
silence, which is immediately broken by an outburst of
praises for Jesus.

He stands up and simply says: ' Thank Mary ' and
withdraws from the banquet. His disciples follow Him. On
the threshold He repeats: 'May peace be in this house
and God's blessing on you .' ' Goodbye, Mother.'

Jesus Drives The Merchants Out Of The Temple

Jesus enters into the Temple complex accompanied by His six disciples; Peter, Andrew, John, James, Philip and Bartholomew, where there is already a large crowd gathered inside as it is also outside the Temple complex. In fact, looking down from the top of the hill on which the Temple stands, the narrow winding streets of Jerusalem are swarming with pilgrims arriving in flocks from every part of town so that the streets look like a moving multi-coloured ribbon between its white houses and the whole town is utterly transformed into a rare toy made of gaily coloured ribbons converging towards the brilliant domes of the House of the Lord.

But inside the complex, it is....a real market. The serenity of the holy place has been destroyed by people running, some calling, some contracting for lambs, shouting and cursing because of the extortionate prices, animals bleating as they are driven into enclosures- rough partitions made of ropes and pegs erected by merchants who stand at the entrance to bargain with buyers.

There are blows with cudgels, bleatings, curses, shouts, insults to servant boys who are not prompt in gathering or selecting the animals, abuses to buyers who haggle over prices or who turn away from a purchase and graver insults still to those who wisely brought their own lambs. There is more bawling by the benches of the money changers where the legal exchange rate has been casually ignored and instead, without there being any fixed rate, the money changers now turned loan sharks, impose extortionate rates to hike up their profits just as they fancy and they do not joke in their transactions! The poorer the people are or the farther afield they come from, the more they are fleeced: the old more than the young and those from beyond Palestine even more than the old folk.

And it is clear that this is always the custom at least at Passover time; that the Temple becomes... a stock exchange or a black market.

A poor old man, one of many, looks gloomily again and again at the money he has saved in a whole year with much hard work. He takes it out and puts it back into his purse dozens and dozens of times, going from one money changer to another and sometimes in the end, returning to the first one, who then avenges himself for their original desertion by raising his commission. And the big coins pass regretfully from the clutches of its sighing owner into the grasping hands of the sharks who change them into smaller coins.

And then the poor old man moves on to another tragedy with the lamb merchants over the choice and payment for the Lambs. And if, as happens time and time again, the poor old man is also half blind then he is fobbed off with the most wretched looking little lamb.

An old couple- man and wife- bring back a poor little lamb, which has been rejected by those who perform the sacrifices as being faulty. The old couple cry and plead with the lamb merchant, who, far from being moved, replies in anger with crude words and cruder manners: 'Considering what you want to spend, Galileans, the lamb I gave you is even too good. Go away! Or if you want a better one, you must pay five more coins. '

'In the name of God! We are poor and old! Are you going to prevent us from celebrating this Passover which may be our last one? Are you not satisfied with what you wanted for a poor little lamb? '

'Go away, you filthy lot. Joseph the Elder is now coming here. I enjoy his favour. God be with you, Joseph! Come and make your choice! '

Joseph the Elder, also known as Joseph of Arimathea, passes by, stately and proud, magnificently dressed, without as much as a glance at the poor old people weeping at the entrance to the enclosure. He enters the enclosure, picks a magnificent lamb and nearly bumps into the old couple as he goes out with his fat, bleating lamb.

Jesus who is now nearby, has also made His purchase, and Peter, who bargained for Him, is pulling a fairly good lamb. Peter would like to go at once where they offer the sacrifices but Jesus turns to the right, towards the dismayed, weeping, undecided old couple, who are knocked about by the crowds and insulted by the vendor. Jesus, Who is so tall that the heads of the poor old souls reach only up to His heart, lays one hand on the shoulder of the woman and asks her: ' Why are you crying, woman? '

The little old woman turns round and she sees the young, tall, stately man, in a beautiful new white tunic and a matching snow-white mantle. She mistakes Him for a doctor because of His garments and His aspect and her surprise is the greater because doctors and priests neither pay attention to the poor nor do they protect them from the stinginess of merchants. She explains to Jesus the reason for their tears.

'Change this lamb for these believers. It is not worthy of
the altar, neither is it fair that you should take advantage
of two poor old people, only because they are weak and
unprotected. 'says Jesus to the lamb vendor.
'And who are You? '
'A just man. '
'By Your way of speaking and Your companions', I know
You are a Galilean. Can there be a just man in Galilee? '
'Do what I told you, and be a just man yourself. '
'Listen! Listen to the Galilean Who is defending His
equals! And He wants to teach us of the Temple! ' The
man laughs and jeers, imitating the Galilean accent,
which is more musical and softer than the Judaean.
Many people draw nearer to them and other merchants
and moneychangers take the side of their fellow
merchant against Jesus.
Amongst the people present there are two or three
ironical rabbis. One of them asks: 'Are You a doctor? ', in
a manner that would try even the patience of Job.
'Yes, I am.'
'What do You teach? '
'This I teach: to make the House of God a house of prayer
and not a usury or a market place. That is what I teach. '
Jesus is formidable. He looks like the archangel on the
threshold of Eden and even without a flashing sword in
His hand, the beams from His eyes strike the impious
mockers like lightning. Jesus has nothing in His hands.
All He has is His wrath. And full of wrath, He walks fast
and solemnly between the money changers› benches: He
scatters the coins that have been so meticulously sorted
according to their values, He overturns the benches and
tables throwing everything onto the ground with great
clattering noises. Amidst the clanging of rebounding
metals and beaten wood, angry cries, shrieks of terror
and shouts of approval rise mingled. But Jesus is not
quite finished yet.

21

He snatches some ropes used to hold oxen, sheep and lambs from the hands of the stable boys and uses them to make a very hard lash with the slip knots that are real scourges. Then He lifts the lash and swings it striking mercilessly with it. Yes....mercilessly.

The unforeseen storm hits heads and backs. The believers move to one side admiring the scene; the guilty ones, chased as far as the external wall, take to their heels, leaving their money on the ground and abandoning their animals in a great confusion of legs, horns and wings, some of which, startled, run and fly away. The bellows of oxen, bleatings of sheep and fluttering of turtle doves and pigeons, add to the bursts of laughter and the shouting of the believers as they mock the escaping credit sharks drown even the plaintive chorus of lambs being slaughtered in another yard.

Priests, rabbis and Pharisees rush to the spot. Jesus is still in the middle of the yard, turning from the chase, the lash still in His hands.

'Who are You? How dare You do that, upsetting the prescribed ceremonies? From which school are You? We do not know You, neither do we know where You come from.'

'I am He Who is Mighty. I can do anything. Destroy this true Temple and I will raise it to give praise to God. I am not upsetting the holiness of the House of God or of the ceremonies, but you upset it by allowing His House to become the centre of credit sharks and merchants. My school is the school of God. The same school the whole of Israel had when the Eternal God spoke to Moses. You do not know Me? You will know Me. You do not know where I come from? You will learn.'

Then ignoring the priests, Jesus turns to the people, standing tall in His white tunic, with His mantle open and blowing in the wind behind His back, His arms outstretched like an orator reinforcing the key point of

his speech, He says: ' Listen, Israel! In Deuteronomy it is said: "You are to appoint judges and scribes at all the gates... and they must administer an impartial judgment to the people. You must be impartial; you must take no bribes, for a bribe blinds wise men's eyes and jeopardizes the cause of the just. Strict justice must be your ideal, so that you may live in rightful possession of the land that Yahweh your God is giving you." '

'Listen, Israel. In Deuteronomy it is said: "The priests and scribes and the whole of the tribe of Levi shall have no share or inheritance with Israel, because they must live on the foods offered to Yahweh and on His dues; they shall have no inheritance among their brothers, because Yahweh will be their inheritance."'

'Listen, Israel. In Deuteronomy it is said: "You must not lend on interest to your brother, whether the lack be of money or food or anything else. You may demand interest on a loan of a foreigner; you will lend without interest to your brother whatever he needs."

The Lord said that. But now you see that in Israel judgments are administered without justice for the poor. They are not inclined to justice, but they are partial with the rich, and to be poor, to be of the common people means to be oppressed. How can the people say: "Our judges are just" when they see that only the mighty ones are respected and satisfied, whereas the poor have no one who will listen to them? How can the people respect the Lord, when they see that the Lord is not respected by those who should respect Him more than everyone else? Does he who infringes the Lord's commandment respect Him? Why then do the priests in Israel possess property and accept bribes from tax- collectors and sinners, who make them offerings to obtain their favours, while they accept gifts to fill their coffers? God is the inheritance of His priests. He, the Father of Israel, is more than a Father to them and provides them with food, as it is just. But not more than what is just. He did not promise money and possessions to His servants of the sanctuary. In eternal life, they will possess Heaven for their justice, as Moses, Elijah, Jacob and Abraham will, but in this world they must have but a linen garment and a diadem of incorruptible gold: purity and charity, and their bodies must be subject to their souls, which are to be subject to the true God, and their bodies are not to be masters over their souls and against God.

I have been asked on what authority I do this. And on what authority do they violate God's command and allow in the shade of the sacred walls usury on their brothers of Israel, who have come to obey the divine command? I have been asked from what school I come and I replied: "From God's school" Yes, Israel, I have come from and I will take you back to that holy and immutable school. Who wants to know the Light, the Truth, the Way, who wants to hear once again the voice of God speaking to his people, let him come to Me. You followed Moses through the deserts, Israel. Follow Me, because I shall lead you through a far worse desert, to the true blessed Land. At God's command, I will draw you to it, across an open sea. I will cure you of all evils lifting up My Sign.

The time of Grace has come. The Prophets expected it and died waiting for it. The Prophets prophesied it and died in that hope. The just have dreamt of it and died comforted by that dream. It is now here. Come. "The Lord is about to judge His people and have mercy on His servants," as He promised through Moses. '

The people crowding round Jesus stand open-mouthed listening to Him. Then they comment on the new Rabbi's words and ask His companions questions. Jesus goes to another yard, separated from the first one only by a porch and His friends follow Him.

Jesus Meets Judas Iscariot And Thomas And Cures Simon The Zealot

It is evening time still during Passover and the town of Jerusalem is crowded with pilgrims hurrying home. Jesus with His six disciples, walk towards the country house set among the thick olive trees, where He is a guest. Judas Thaddeus, who had wanted to come to Jerusalem with Jesus, is not present.

From the rustic open space in front of the house, A terraced hill covered in olive trees slopes down to a little water torrent flowing along a valley formed by two hills at the top of which there is the Temple on the one whilst the other is covered only with olive trees. Jesus has just begun to climb up the peaceful slope of the hill of olive trees when an elderly man, possibly the farmer or owner of the olive grove approaches the group and addresses himself to John, his manner familiar.

'John, there are two men awaiting your friend.'

'Where are they? Who are they? '

'I don't know. One is certainly Judaean. The other... I don't know. I didn't ask him.'

'Where are they?'

'In the kitchen, waiting, and... and... yes... there is
another man who is all covered with sores. I made him
stay over there, because I am afraid he may be a leper.
He says he wants to see the Prophet Who spoke in the
Temple.'

Jesus, Who has been silent, says: 'Let us go to him first.
Tell the others to come if they so wish. I will speak to
them there, in the olive-grove.

'And He makes for the place indicated by the man.

'And what about us? What shall we do? 'Asks Peter.

'Come, if you want.'

A man, muffled up, is leaning against the rustic wall
supporting the terrace nearest to the property boundary.
He must have reached it via a path along the torrent.
When he sees Jesus approaching him, he shouts: 'Go
back. Back! Have mercy on me!' And he bares his trunk
dropping his tunic to the ground. His face is covered with
scabs but his trunk is one big sore that in places have
become deep wounds, some of which look like burns
whilst others are whitish and glossy, as if there is a thin
white pane of glass on them.

'Are you a leper? What do you want of Me? '

'Don't curse me! Don't stone me. I have been told that
the other evening You revealed Yourself as the Voice of
God and the Bearer of Grace. I was also told that You
gave assurance that by raising Your Sign, You will cure
all diseases. Please raise it on me. I have come from the
sepulchres... over there... I crept like a snake amongst
the bushes near the torrent to arrive here without being
seen. I waited until evening before leaving because at
dusk it is more difficult to see who I am. I dared... I

found this man, the man of the house, he is good. He did not kill me. He only said: "Wait over there, near the little wall." Have mercy on me.'

Jesus goes nearer to the leper but the six disciples together with the landlord and the two strangers stay far back and look disgusted.

'Don't come nearer. Don't! I am infected!' cries the leper but Jesus comes closer still. He looks at the leper so mercifully, that the man begins to cry and kneeling down with his face almost touching the ground, he moans: 'Your Sign! Your Sign!'

'It will be raised when it is time. But now I say to you: Stand up. Be healed. I want it. And be the sign in this town that must recognize Me. Rise, I say. And do not sin, out of gratitude to God!' Slowly, the man rises, seeming to emerge from the long flowery grass as from a shroud... and is healed. He looks at himself in the last dim light of the day. He is healed. He shouts:

'I am clean! Oh! What shall I do for You now?'

'You must comply with the Law. Go to the priest. Be good in future. Go.'

The man is about to throw himself at Jesus' feet, but remembering that he is still unclean according to the Law, restrains himself and instead kisses his own hand, and throws a kiss to Jesus and weeps. He weeps out of joy.

The others are dumbfounded.

Jesus turns away from the healed man and rouses them smiling. 'My friends, it was only leprosy of the flesh. But you will see leprosy fall from hearts. Is it you that wanted Me? 'He asks the two strangers. 'Here I am. Who are

29

you?'

'We heard You the other evening... in the Temple. We looked for You in town. A man, who said he is a relative of Yours, told us You stay here.'

'Why are you looking for Me?'

'To follow You, if You will allow us, because You have words of truth.'

'Follow Me? But do you know where I am going?'

'No, Master, but certainly to glory.'

'Yes. But not to a glory of this world. I am going to a glory which is in Heaven and is conquered by virtue and sacrifice. Why do you want to follow Me?' He asks them again.

'To take part in Your glory.'

'According to Heaven?'

'Yes, according to Heaven.'

'Not everybody is able to arrive there because Mammon lays more snares for those who yearn for Heaven than for the rest. And only he who has strong will power can resist. Why follow Me, if to follow Me would mean a continuous struggle against the enemy, which is in us, against the hostile world, and against the Enemy who is Satan?'

'Because that is the desire of our souls, which have been conquered by You. You are holy and powerful. We want to be Your friends.'

'Friends!!!' Jesus is silent and sighs. Then He stares at the one who has been the spokesman and who has now removed the mantle-hood from his head, and is bareheaded. 'Who are you? You speak better than a man of the people.'

'I am Judas, the son of Simon. I come from Kerioth. But I am of the Temple. I am waiting for and dreaming of the King of the Jews. I heard You speak like a king. I saw Your kingly gestures. Take me with You.'

'Take you? Now? At once? No.'

'Why not, Master?'

'Because it is better to examine ourselves carefully before venturing on very steep roads.'

'Do You not believe I am sincere?'

'You have said it. I believe in your impulsiveness. But I do not believe in your perseverance. Think about it, Judas. I am going away now and I will be back for Pentecost. If you are in the Temple, you will see Me. Examine yourself. And who are you? '.

'I am another one who saw You. I would like to be with You. But now I am frightened. '

'No. Presumption ruins people. Fear may be an impediment, but it is a help when it originates from humility. Do not be afraid. Think about it, too, and when I come back... '

'Master, You are so holy! I am afraid of not being worthy. Nothing else. Because I do not doubt my love... '

'What is your name? '

'Thomas of Didymus. '

'I will remember your name. Go in peace. '

Jesus dismisses them and He goes into the hospitable house for supper.

The six disciples with Him want to know many things. 'Why, Master, why did You treat them differently? Because there was a difference. Both of them had the same impulsiveness... 'Asks John.

'My friend, also the same impulsiveness may have a different taste and bring about a different effect. They both certainly had the same impulsiveness. But they were not the same in their purpose. And the one who appears less perfect is, in fact, more perfect, because he has no incentive to human glory. He loves Me because he loves Me. '

'And so do I. '

'And I, too. ', 'And I. ', 'And I. ', 'And I. ', 'And I. '

'I know. I know you for what you are. '

'Are we therefore perfect? '

'Oh! No! But, like Thomas, you will become perfect if you persevere in your desire to love. Perfect?! Oh! My friends! And who is perfect but God? '

'You are! '

'I solemnly tell you that I am not perfect by Myself, if you think I am a prophet. No man is perfect. But I am perfect because He Who is speaking to you is the Word of the Father: part of God. His thought that becomes Word. I have Perfection in Myself. And you must believe Me to be such if you believe that I am the Word of the Father. And yet, see, My friends, I want to be called the Son of man because I lower Myself taking upon Myself all the miseries of man, to bear them as My first scaffold, and cancel them, after bearing them, without suffering from them Myself. What a burden, My friends! But I bear it with joy. It is a joy for Me to bear it, because, since I am the Son of mankind, I will make mankind once again the child of God. As it was on the first day. '

The six disciple, Jesus and the Landlord are seated evenly at a long narrow table in a low wide dimly lit kitchen with dark smoky walls. The room is dimly lit by a small oil lamp on the rustic table that reveals the faces of those sitting around it and also, the three legged stools, real country furniture, on which they are all seated.

Jesus speaks very gently, gesticulating calmly with His hands on the table, His head slightly inclined to one side, His face lit up from below. He smiles gently, He Who shortly before, was so majestic a Master in His bearing, is now friendly in His gestures. His disciples listen to Him closely.

'Master... why did Your cousin not come, even though he knows where You live?'

'My Peter!... You will be one of My stones, the first one. But not all the stones can be easily used. Have you seen the marble blocks in the Praetorium building? With hard labour they were torn away from the bosom of the mountain side, and are now part of the Praetorium. Look instead at those stones down there shining in the moonlight, in the water of the Kidron. They arrived in the river- bed by themselves, and if anyone wants to take them, they do not put up any resistance. My cousin is like the first stones I am speaking of... The bosom of the mountain side: his family, they contend for him with Me.'

'But I want to be exactly like the stones in the torrent. I am quite prepared to

Leave everything for You: home, wife, fishing, brothers. Everything, Rabboni, for You. '

'I know, Peter. That is why I love you. Also Judas will come. '

'Who? Judas of Kerioth? I don't care for him. He is a dandy young man, but... I prefer... I myself prefer... 'They all laugh at Peter's witty remark. '... There is nothing to laugh at. I mean that I prefer a sincere Galilean, a rough fisherman, but without any fraud to... to townsfolk who... I don't know... here: the Master knows what I mean. '

'Yes, I know. But do not judge. We need one another in this world; the good are mixed with the wicked, just like flowers in a field. Hemlock grows beside the salutary mallow. '

'I would like to ask one thing... '

'What, Andrew? '

'John told me about the miracle You worked at Cana... We were hoping so much that You would work one at Capernaum... and You said that You would not work any miracles before fulfilling the Law. Why Cana then? And why here and not in Your own fatherland? '

'To obey the Law is to be united to God and that increases our capabilities. A miracle is the proof of the union with God, as well as of God's benevolent and assenting presence. That is why I wanted to perform My duty as an Israelite, before starting the series of miracles. '

'But You were not bound to fulfil the Law. '

'Why? As the Son of God, I was not. But as a son of the Law, yes, I was. For the time being, Israel knows Me only as such... and, even later, almost everyone in Israel will know Me as such, nay, even less. But I do not want to scandalize Israel and therefore I obey the Law. '

'You are holy. '

'Holiness does not bar obedience. Nay it makes obedience perfect. Besides everything else, there is a good example to be given. What would you say of a father, of an elder brother, of a teacher, of a priest who did not give good examples? '

'And what about Cana? '

'Cana was to make My Mother happy. Cana is the advance due to My Mother. She anticipates Grace. Here I honour the Holy City, making her, in public, the starting point of My power as Messiah. But there, at Cana, I paid honour to the Holy Mother of God, Full of Grace. The world received Me through Her. It is only fair that My first miracle in the world should be for Her. '

There is a knocking at the door then, Thomas returning, enters and throws himself at Jesus' feet.

'Master... I cannot wait until You come back. Let me come with You. I am full of faults, but I have my love, my only real great treasure. It is Yours, it's for You. Let me come, Master... '

Jesus lays His hand on Thomas' head. 'You may stay, Didymus. Follow Me. Blessed are those who are sincere and persistent in their will. You are all blessed. You are more than relatives to Me, because you are My children and My brothers, not according to the blood that dies but according to the will of God and to your spiritual wishes. Now I tell you that I have no closer relative than those who do the will of My Father, and you do it because you want what is good. '

Thomas Becomes A Disciple

'Stand up, My friend. Have you had any supper yet? '
says Jesus to Thomas, moving His hand from Thomas's
head to his shoulder.
' No, Master. I walked a few yards with the other fellow
who was with me, then I left him and I came back saying
that I wanted to speak to the healed leper... I said that
because I thought he would disdain approaching an
impure man. I guessed right. But I wanted to see You,
not the leper... I wanted to say to You: "Please take me"...
I wandered up and down the olive-grove until a young
man asked me what I was doing. He must have thought I
was ill-disposed. He was near a pillar, at the boundary of
the olive-grove. '

'It's my son... ' the landlord explains, smiling ' ...He is on
guard at the oil mill. In the caves under the mill, we still
have almost all the crop of the year. It was a very good
one and we made a lot of oil. And when there are large
crowds about, robbers always get together to plunder
unguarded places. Eight years ago, just at Parasceve,
they robbed us of everything. Since then we keep a good
watch one night each. His mother has gone to take him
his supper. '
'Well, he asked me: "What do you want?", and he spoke
in such a tone that to save my back from his stick, I
answered at once: "I am looking for the Master Who lives
here". Then he replied: "If what you say is true, come to
the house". And he brought me here. It was he who
knocked at the door and he did not go away until he
heard my first words. '
'Do you live far away? '
'I live on the other side of the town, near the Eastern
Gate. '
'Are you alone? '
'I was with some relatives. But they have gone to stay
with other relatives on the road to Bethlehem. I remained
here to look for You day and night, until I found You. '

Jesus smiles and says: ' So no one is waiting for you? '
'No, Master. '
'It is a long way, it is a dark night, the Roman patrols are
about the town. I say: stay with us, if you wish. '
'Oh! Master! ' exhales Thomas, happy.
'Make room for him. And each of us will give something
to our brother. ' Jesus gives him the portion of cheese He
had in front of Him and explains to Thomas: ' We are
poor and our supper is almost over. But there is so much
heart in who offers. ' And He says to John who is sitting
beside Him: ' Give your seat to our friend. '
John gets up at once and sits down at the end of the
table near the landlord.
'Sit down, Thomas, and eat. ' And then He says to them
all: ' You will always behave like that, My friends,
according to the law of charity. A pilgrim is already
protected by the law of God. But now, in My name, you
must love him even more. When anyone asks you for
some bread, a drop of water or a shelter in the name of
God, you must give it in the same name. And you will
receive your reward from God. You must behave so with
everybody. Even with your enemies. And that is the new
Law. Up till now you were told: "Love those who love you
and hate your enemies." I say: "Love also those who hate
you." Oh! if you only knew how much you will be loved by
God, if you love as I am telling you! And when anyone
says: "I want to be your companion in serving the true
Lord God and following His Lamb", then he must be
dearer to you than a brother by blood, because you will
be joined by an eternal bond: the bond of Christ. '
'But if someone comes who is not sincere? It is easy to
say: "I want to do this or that." But words do not always
correspond to the truth ' says Peter, somewhat irritated
and clearly not in his usual jovial mood.
'Peter, listen. What you say is sensible and fair. But, see:
it is better to exceed in bounty and trust rather than
exceed in distrust and hardness. If you help an

undeserving person, what harm will befall you? None.
Nay, God's reward will always be active for you, whereas
the person will be guilty of betraying your trust. '
'No harm? Eh! Very often a worthless person is not
satisfied with ingratitude, but goes much further, even to
the extreme of ruining one's reputation, wealth and one's
very life. '
'True. But would that diminish your merit? No, it would
not. Even if the whole world should believe slander, even
if you became poorer than Job, even if the cruel person
should take your life, what would change in the eyes of
God?
Nothing. Nay, something would change, but to your
advantage because God would add the merits of your
intellectual, financial and physical martyrdom to the
merits of your bounty '
'All right! Perhaps it is so. ' agrees Peter and, still sulking,
he rests his head on his hand. Jesus addresses Thomas:
'My friend, before, in the olive- grove I said to you: "When
I come back here, if you are still willing, you will be one
of My disciples." Now I say to you: "Are you willing to do
Jesus a favour?"'
'Most certainly. '
'And if this favour should cost you some sacrifice? '
'There is no sacrifice in serving You. What is it You want?
'
'I wanted to say... but you may have some business,
some affections...'
'None, none! I have You! Tell me. '
'Listen. Tomorrow at daybreak the leper will leave the
sepulchres to find someone who will inform the priest.
You will be the first to go to the sepulchres. It is charity.
And you will shout: "Come out, you, the one who was
cleansed yesterday. I have been sent by Jesus of
Nazareth, the Messiah of Israel, He who cleansed you."
Let the world of the "living dead" know My name, let them
throb with hope, and let those come to Me, who will have

faith in addition to hope, that I may heal them. It is the
first form of purity that I am bringing, the first form of
the resurrection, of which I am the lord. One day I will
grant a greater purity... One day the sealed tombs will
violently expel those who are really dead, and they will
appear and laugh with their empty eye sockets, with their
bare jaws, because of the rejoicing of the souls freed from
Limbo, a remote rejoicing and yet perceived even by
skeletons. They will appear to laugh because of this
liberation and to throb knowing it is due to... Go! He will
come to you. You will do what he asks you to do; assist
him in everything, as if he were your brother, and also
say to him: "When you are completely purified, we will go
together along the road of the river, beyond Doco and
Ephraim. Jesus, the Master, will be waiting for us to tell
us in what we have to serve him." '
'I will do that. And what about the other one? '
'Who? The Iscariot? '
'Yes, Master. '
'The advice I gave him still stands. Let him decide by
himself and let him take a long time. Nay, avoid seeing
him. I will be with the leper. Only lepers wander about in
the valley of the sepulchres and those who pitifully are in
touch with them. '
Peter mumbles something. Jesus hears him. 'What is the
matter with you, Peter? You either grumble or are silent.
You seem to be dissatisfied. Why? '
'I am dissatisfied. We were the first and You did not work
a miracle for us. We were the first and You let a stranger
sit beside You. We were the first and You entrust him, not
us, with a task. We were the first and... yet, yes, we seem
to be the last ones. Why are You going to wait for them
on the road near the river? Certainly to entrust them
with some mission. Why them, and not us? '
Jesus looks at Peter and smiles as him as smiles at a
child. He gets up, walks slowly over to Peter and, smiling,
says to him: 'Peter! Peter! You are a big, old baby! ' Then

turning to Andrew who was beside his brother, Jesus says ' Go and take My seat ' . Then Jesus sits Himself beside Peter, clasping Peter's shoulders with His arm and holding him against His own shoulder, He says 'Peter, you think I am being unfair, but I am not. On the contrary it is a proof that I know what you are worth. Look. Who needs proofs? He who is not yet certain. I knew you were so certain about Me, that I did not feel any need to give you evidence of My power. Proofs are required here in Jerusalem, where souls have been deemed by vices, irreligiousness, politics and many worldly things to such an extent that they can no longer see the Light passing by. But up there, on our beautiful lake, so clear under a clear sky, amongst honest and good willing people, no proof is required. You will have miracles. I will pour torrents of graces upon you. But consider how I valued you, I took you without exacting any proof and without finding it necessary to give you any, because I know who you are. You are dear to Me, so dear, and so faithful. '

Peter cheers up: 'Forgive me, Jesus. '

'Yes, I forgive you because your sulkiness is a sign of love. But do not be envious any more, Simon of Jonas. Do you know what the heart of your Jesus is? Have you ever seen the sea, the real sea? You have? Well, My heart is bigger than the immense sea! And there is room for everybody. For the whole of mankind. And the smallest person has a place exactly as the greatest. And a sinner finds love just like an innocent. I am entrusting these with a mission. Certainly. Do you want to forbid Me? I chose you. You did not choose yourselves. I am therefore free to decide how I want to employ you. And if I leave them here with a mission – which might well be a test, as the lapse of time granted to the Iscariot may be due to mercy – can you reproach Me? How do you know that I am not saving a greater mission for you? And is not the nicest mission to be told: "You will come with me"? '

'It is true. I am a blockhead! Forgive me... '

'Yes. I forgive everything. Oh! Peter!... But I beg you all never to discuss merits and positions. I could have been born a king. I was born poor, in a stable. I could have been rich. I lived with My work and now I live out of charity. And yet, believe Me, My friends, there is no one greater than I in the eyes of God. Greater than I am, Who am here: the servant of man. '

'You a servant? Never! '

'Why not, Peter? '

'Because I will serve You. '

'Even if You served Me as a mother serves her child, I have come to serve man. I will be a Saviour for him. What service is there like that? '

'Oh! Master! You explain everything. And what seemed dark becomes clear at once! '

'Are you happy now, Peter? Now let Me finish talking to Thomas. Are you sure you will recognize the leper? He is the only one healed; but he may already have left by starlight, to find an early wayfarer. And someone, anxious to enter the town and see his relatives, might perhaps take his place. Listen to his description. I was near him and I saw him well in the twilight. He is tall and thin. Of a dark complexion, like a cross breed, very deep and dark eyes with snow white eyebrows, hair as white as linen and somewhat curly, and a long snubbed nose like the Libyans', two thick protruding lips particularly the lower one. He is so olive-coloured that his lips verge on violet. He has an old scar on his forehead and it will be the only stain, now that he has been cleansed from scabs and dirt. '

'He must be old, if he is all white. '

'No, Philip, he looks old, but he is not. Leprosy made him white. '

'What is he? A cross-breed? '

'Perhaps, Peter. He resembles African people. '

'Will he be an Israelite, then? '

'We will find out. But suppose he is not? '
'Eh! If he were not, he would go away. He is already lucky that he deserved to be healed. '
'No, Peter. Even if he is an idolater, I will not send him away. Jesus has come for everybody. And I solemnly tell you that people living in darkness will overcome the children of the people of Light... '
Jesus sighs, stands up and thanks the Father with a hymn and then blesses everyone.

Judas Of Alphaeus, Thomas And Simon Are Accepted As Disciples At The Jordan

We are once more on the beautiful banks of the river Jordan, that resound with the solemn green- blue peace of its gentle flowing waters and leafy branches as a sweet melody. The flow of the water is so gentle that only the rustling of the reed thickets along the gravel bed, the rise and fall of the long ribbon-like leaves of the canes dipping and lulling in the water and also the graceful caressing and combing of the thin green flexible foliage of a cluster of willows, stretching them softly on the surface of the water.
The peace and quiet of this early morning is broken only by the warbling of birds and the rustling of water and leaves. Dew drops glitter on the tall green grass between the trees, grass that is only recently grown after the recent nourishing spring showers.

On a well-kept Roman military road that runs through various regions to the capital, separated from the river Jordan by woodland that serves to consolidate the river banks and contain the water in times of flood. The woodland also continues on the other side of the road so that the road looks like a tunnel with a roof of interlacing leafy branches that give welcome protection to travellers on foot, in the hot climate.

At one point along the river, it forms a wide bend, followed also by the road so the leafy embankment seems a huge green barrier that encloses a basin of even calmer waters, giving it the appearance of a lake in a luxury park.

In the middle of the bend, three travellers on foot, Thomas, Judas Thaddeus and the healed leper, Simon, stand waiting. They look anxiously up to the north towards Samaria and then down to the south, towards Jerusalem. And then they look anxiously, expectantly between the trees and speak amongst themselves.
'Can you see anything? '
'No, I can't.'
'Neither can I.'
'And yet this is the place. '
'Are you sure? '
'I'm sure, Simon. One of the six said to me, when the Master was going away amid the acclamations of the crowd, after the miraculous healing of a crippled beggar at the Fish Gate: "We are now going out of Jerusalem. Wait for us five miles between Jericho and Doco, at the bend of the river, along the road in the woodland." This one. He also said: "We will be there in three days' time at dawn." This is the third day, and we were here before dawn. '
'Will He come? Perhaps we should have followed Him from Jerusalem. '
'You were not yet allowed to mix with the crowds, Simon.
'
'If my cousin told you to come here, He will certainly come here. He always keeps His promise. All we can do is wait.'

'Have you always been with Him? '
'Yes, always. Since He came back to Nazareth, He was my good companion. We were always together. We are about

the same age, I am a little older. And I was the favourite
of His father, who was my father's brother. Also His
Mother was very fond of me. I grew up more with Her
than with my own mother. '
'She was fond... Is She no longer as fond of you, now? '
'Oh! Yes, She is. But we have parted a little since He
became a prophet. My relatives are not happy about it. '
'Which relatives? '
'My father and the two older brothers. The other one is
undecided... My father is very old and I did not have the
courage to hurt him. But now... Now, no longer so. Now I
am going where my heart and my mind tell me. I am
going to Jesus. I don't think I am offending the Law by
doing so. In any case... if what I want to do was not right,
Jesus would tell me. I will do what He says. Is it right for
a father to prevent a son from doing good? If I feel that
my salvation is there, why prevent me from reaching it?
Why, at times, are our fathers our enemies? '
Simon sighs, as one overwhelmed by sad memories, and
lowers his head, but does not speak.
'I have already overcome the obstacle....' says Thomas.
'...My father listened to me and he understood me. He
blessed me and said "Go. May this Passover be for you
the liberation from the slavery of waiting. You are
fortunate because you can believe. I will wait. But if it is
really 'Him', and you will find out following Him, then
come and say to your old father: 'Come, Israel has the
Expected One' ". '
'You are luckier than I am. And we always lived beside
Him! And we, in the family, do not believe!... We say, that
is: they say: "He has gone mad!"'
'There, there is a group of people ' shouts Simon. 'It's
Him, it's Him! I recognise His fair head! Oh! Come! Let us
run! 'They start walking fast heading south. When they
reach the centre of the bend, the trees cover the
remainder of the road, so that the two groups meet,
facing each other unexpectedly. Jesus seems to be

coming up from the river, because He is among the trees
on the bank.
'Master! ' ' Jesus! ' ' My Lord! '
The three cries of the disciple, the cousin and the cured
leper are full of joy and veneration.
'Peace to you! 'Comes the beautiful, unmistakable, full,
resonant, calm, expressive, clear, virile, sweet, incisive
voice of the Master! 'You too, Judas, My cousin, are here?
'

They embrace each other. Judas is weeping.
'Why are you weeping? '
'Oh! Jesus! I want to stay with You! '
'I have been waiting for you all the time. Why did you not
come? 'Judas bows his head and is silent.
'They did not let you! And now? '
'Jesus, I... I cannot obey them. I want to obey only You.'
'But I did not give you an order. '
'No, You did not. But it is Your mission that gives it! It is
He, Who sent You, Who is speaking here, in my heart,
and says to me: "Go to Him". It is She, Who bore You, my
sweet teacher, Who with Her gentle look, as mild as a
dove's, says to me without uttering a word: "Be of
Jesus!". Can I ignore that heavenly voice that pierces my
heart? Can I ignore the prayers of such a Holy Woman,
Who implores me for my own good? Only because I am
Your cousin on Joseph's side, am I not to acknowledge
You for what You are, whereas the Baptist recognized
You, although he had never seen You, here, on the banks
of this river and he greeted You as the "Lamb of God"?
And I, should I not be capable of anything, although I
was brought up with You, and I was good because I
followed You, and I became a son of the Law through
Your Mother, from Whom I learned not only the six
hundred and thirteen precepts of the rabbis, besides the
Scriptures and the prayers, but also the essence of them
all? '
'And your father? '

'My father? He does not lack bread and assistance, and then... you give me the example. You have thought of the welfare of the people, rather than the little advantage of Mary. And She is alone. Tell me, Master, is it not right for a son to say to his father, without lacking respect: "Father, I love you. But God is above you and I will follow Him"? '

'Judas, My cousin and My friend, I tell you: you have made good progress on the way to Light. Come. It is lawful to speak thus to a father, when it is God Who calls. There is nothing above God. Also the laws of relationship cease, that is they are raised to a dignity, because with our tears, we give our fathers and mothers a greater help and for something that lasts forever, not just for the short time in this world. We draw them with us to Heaven by sacrificing our affections, to God. So, Judas, stay here. I have been waiting for you and I am happy to have you, the friend of My life at Nazareth. '

Judas is touched.

Jesus addresses Thomas: 'You obeyed faithfully. That is the first virtue of a disciple. '

'I came because I want to be faithful to You.'

'And you will be. I tell you. And you, who are hiding shyly in the shade, come here. Do not be afraid. '

'My Lord! ' And Simon throws at Jesus' feet.

'Stand up. Your name? '

'Simon. '

'Your family? '

'My Lord... it was powerful... I was powerful too... But bitter sectarian hatred... and errors of youth damaged its power. My father... Oh! I must speak ill of him, who caused me so many earthly tears! You see, You saw the gift he gave me. '

'Was he a leper? '

'He was not. Neither was I. But he suffered from another disease which we in Israel associate with various forms of leprosy. He... his caste was then triumphant; he lived

and died as a powerful man, at home. I... if You had not saved me, I would have died in the valley of sepulchres. '
'Are you alone? '
'Yes, I am. I have a faithful servant who looks after what property is left. I sent word to him. '
'And your mother? '
'She... is dead. 'And Simon seems embarrassed.
Jesus looks at him attentively. 'Simon, you asked me: "What shall I do for You?" Now I say to you: "Follow Me."'
'I will, at once, my Lord... But... But I... let me tell You one thing. I am, I was called "Zealot" because of the caste, and "Cananean", because of my mother. See. I am of a dark complexion. In my veins there is the blood of a slave woman. My father had no children by his wife, and he had me by a slave girl. His wife was a good woman and she brought me up as her own son and she took care of me in my endless illnesses until she died... '
'There are no slaves or freemen in the eyes of God. There is only one slavery in His eyes: sin. And I have come to abolish it. I am calling everybody, because the Kingdom is for all men. Are you a learned man? '
'Yes, I am. I also had my position amongst the important people, as long as my disease was hidden under my clothes. But when it spread to my face... My enemies then could not believe they were at last able to confine me amongst the "dead", although a Roman doctor of Caesarea, when I consulted him, told me that mine was not real leprosy, but hereditary serpigo*, which I would spread only by procreation. Is it possible for me not to curse my father? '
* ringworm
'You must not curse him. He has caused you all sorts of trouble... '
'Yes, he did! He was a squanderer, a vicious, cruel, heartless man without any love. He deprived me of my health, he denied me love and peace, he branded me with a shameful name and with a disease which is a mark of

51

infamy... He wanted everything for himself, even his son's future. He deprived me of everything, also of the joy of being a father. '

'That is why I say to you: "Follow Me". As My follower you will find father and children. Look up, Simon. There, the True Father is smiling at you. Look at the wide world, at the continents, at the countries: there are children and children everywhere; children of the souls for the childless. They are waiting for you, and many like you are also waiting. There are no foundlings under My Sign. There is no solitude, no difference in My Sign. It is a sign of love, and it gives love. Come, My childless Simon. Come, Judas, who are losing your father for My sake. I join you in the same destiny. '

They are both beside Him and He is holding His hands on their shoulders as if He were taking possession of them and imposing a common yoke on them. 'And I unite you together.....' He says '.... But now I will separate you. Simon, you will stay here with Thomas. You will prepare with him the way for My return: I will be back soon, and I want the people to be waiting for Me. Tell the sick people that He Who can cure their illnesses, is about to come here: you can certainly tell them that. Tell those who are waiting, that the Messiah is among His people. Tell the sinners that He Who forgives has come to give them strength to rise... '

'Will we be able to do that? '

'Yes, you will. All you have to say is: "He has come. He calls you. He is waiting for you. He has come to grant you graces. Come here to see Him", and to these words, add a report of what you know. And you, Judas, My cousin, come with Me and these. But you will stay at Nazareth. '

'Why, Jesus? '

'Because you must prepare My way in My fatherland. Do you think it is a small mission? I can tell you that there is not a harder one... ' Jesus sighs.

'And will I succeed? '

'You will and you will not. But it will be sufficient to be justified. '

'Justified of what? And with whom? '

'With God. With your fatherland. With your family. They will not be able to reproach us, because we offered good things: and if the fatherland and the family will disdain our offer, we shall not be blamed for their loss. '

'And what about us? '

'You, Peter? You will go back to your fishing nets. '

'Why? '

'Because I will teach you slowly and I will take you with Me, when I find that you are ready. '

'But will we see You, then? '

'Certainly. I will often come to see you, or I will send for you when I am at Capernaum. Now, let us say goodbye, My friends and let us go. I bless you, who are staying here. May My peace be with You. '

Return To Nazareth After Passover With The Six Disciples

Jesus is on His way home to Nazareth accompanied by His Cousin, Judas Thaddeus and also His six disciples. From the top of the hill where they are, they can see the white village amongst the green of the trees, with its houses scattered up and down the sweetly undulating slopes that gently decline in some places and is steeper in others.

'Here we are, My friends. That is My house. My Mother is at home because there is smoke rising from the house. Perhaps She is baking. I will not ask you to stay with Me, because I imagine you will be anxious to go to your homes. But if you wish to share My bread with Me and meet My Mother, Whom John has already met, then I say to You: "Come". '

The six disciples, who were already sad because of the impending separation, all cheer up again and accept the invitation wholeheartedly.

'Let us go, then. '

They descend the hillock quickly and take to the main road. It air is still warm but the day has turned to evening and the shades of evening are falling over the country, where the crops are beginning to ripen.

As they enter the village, there are women going to and fro between the fountain and their homes. Men standing on the threshold of their little workshops or working in

their kitchen gardens wave to Jesus and Judas and they
pass by and the children press round Jesus and chatter:
'Have You come back? ',
 'Are You staying here, now? '
'The wheel of my little barrow is broken again.'
'Do You know, Jesus. I have a new baby sister, and they
have called her Mary.'
'The schoolmaster told me that I have learned everything
and that I am a true son of the Law.'
'Sarah is not here, because her mother is very ill. She
cries, because she is afraid. ',
'My brother Isaac got married. We had a lovely feast.'
Jesus listens, caresses, praises, promises His help.
And they reach the house thus. Mary is already waiting
at the door, as She has been informed by thoughtful boy.
'Son! '
'Mother! '
And Mother and Son are in each other's arms. Mary, Who
is much smaller than Jesus, is leaning with Her head
on Her Son's chest, clasped in His arms. He kisses Her
blond hair.

And then they enter the house.
The disciples, including Judas, remain outside, to give
Jesus and Mary a few moments of privacy.
'Jesus! My Son! ' and Mary's voice trembles, as one
choked with sobs.
'Why, Mother, why are You so upset? '
'Oh! Son. They told Me... In the Temple, that day, there
were some Galileans and some Nazarenes... They came
back... and they told Me... Oh! Son! '
'But You can see, Mother, that I am well. I suffered no
harm. God was glorified in His House.'
'Yes, I know, Son of My heart. I know it was like the
blare awaking the sleepers. And I am happy for the
glory given to God... I am happy that this people of Mine
awake to God... I am not reproaching You... I will not be

a hindrance to You... I understand You and... and I am happy, but I begot You, Son!... ' Mary is still clasped by Jesus' arms and She has spoken holding Her little open hands pressed against Her Son's chest, Her head turned up towards Him, Her eyes shining with tears ready to run down Her cheeks. Now She is silent, leaning Her head on His chest and She looks like a grey turtle-dove, in Her greyish dress, sheltered by two strong white wings, because Jesus is wearing His white tunic and mantle. 'Mother! Poor Mother! Dear Mother!... ' Jesus kisses Her again. Then He says ' Well, see? I am here, but I am not alone. I have My first disciples with Me, and the others are in Judaea. Also My cousin Judas is with Me and follows Me... '

'Judas? '

'Yes, Judas. I know why You are surprised. Among those who told You what happened, there certainly was Alphaeus with his sons, and I am not mistaken if I tell You that they criticised Me. But do not be afraid. Today it is so, tomorrow will be different. A man is to be cultivated like the soil, and where there are thorns, there will also be roses. Judas, of whom You are so fond, is already with Me. '

'Where is he now? '

'Outside with the others. Have You got enough bread for everybody? '

'Yes, Son. Mary of Alphaeus is taking it out of the oven just now. Mary is very good to Me, particularly now. '

'God will give her glory. ' He goes to the door and calls: ' Judas! Your mother is here! Come in, My friends! '

They go in and greet Jesus' Mother. Judas kisses Her and then runs off to look for his mother.

John, who has already met Mary, speaks to Her immediately after Judas, bowing down to Her and receiving Her blessing.

Then, Jesus introduces the other five disciples by name: Peter, Andrew, James, Nathanael, Philip.

Mary greets them and asks them to sit down. She is
the landlady and although adoring Her Jesus with Her
glances – Her soul seems to be speaking to Her Son
through Her eyes – She takes care of Her guests. She
would like to bring some water to refresh them. But Peter
objects: 'No, Woman. I cannot allow that.
Please sit near Your Son, Holy Mother. I will go, we will
all go into the kitchen garden to refresh ourselves. '
Mary of Alphaeus rushes in, flushed and covered with
flour and she greets Jesus Who blesses her. Then
she leads the six men into the kitchen garden, to the
fountain, and comes back happy. 'Oh! Mary! ' she says to
the Virgin. 'Judas told me. How happy I am! For Judas
and for You, my dear sister-in-law. I know that the others
will scold me. But it does not matter. I will be happy the
day I know that they are all for Jesus. We are mothers
and we know... we feel what is good for our children. And
I feel that You, Jesus, are the wealth of my children.'
Jesus caresses her head and smiles at her.
The disciples come back in and Mary of Alphaeus serves
them sweet-smelling bread, olives and cheese. Then she
brings a small amphora of red wine, which Jesus pours
out to his friends. It is always Jesus Who offers and then
hands things out. At first the disciples are somewhat
embarrassed, then they become surer of themselves
and they speak about their houses, of the journey to
Jerusalem, of the miracles that Jesus has worked. They
are full of zeal and affection and Peter tries to form an
alliance with Mary so that Jesus will take him at once so
he does not have to wait at Bethsaida.
'Do what He tells you ' urges Mary, with a gentle smile.
'The wait will be more useful to you than an immediate
union. Whatever My Jesus does is always well done.'
Peter's hope vanishes but he submits with good grace,
only asking' Will it be a long wait?'
 Jesus smiles at him, but says nothing more.
Mary interprets Jesus' smile as a favourable sign and

She explains: 'Simon of Jonas, He is smiling... I therefore say to you: as fast as a swallow's flight over the lake will be the time of your obedient waiting.'
'Thank You, Woman.'
'Have you nothing to say, Judas? And you, John? '
'I am looking at You, Mary.'
'And I.'
'I am also looking at you... and do you know? This reminds Me of bygone days. Also then I had three pairs of eyes staring at Me lovingly. Do you remember, Mary, My three pupils?'
'Oh! I do remember! You are quite right! And even now, three of almost the same age, are looking at You with all their love. And I think that John is like Jesus, as Jesus was then, so fair and rosy, the youngest of them all. 'The others are anxious to know more... and memories and stories of the past are awakened and related as it grows dark outside.

'My friends, I have no bedrooms. But the workshop where I used to work is over there. If you wish to take shelter there... But there is nothing but benches in it. '
'A comfortable bed for fishermen, wont to sleep on narrow boards. Thank You, Master. It is an honour and a blessing to sleep under Your roof.'
They bid good night and withdraw. Judas also goes home with his mother leaving Jesus and Mary in the room, sitting on the chest, in the light of the little oil lamp, each with one arm round the other's shoulder, and Jesus tells Mary of His recent journey. And Mary listens blissful, anxious, happy.

Cure Of A Blind Man At Capernaum

It is a beautiful summer sunset; the whole of the western
sky is alight with the glare of the setting sun and Lake of
Gennesaret (also known as lake Tiberias or lake Galilee)
looks like a huge disc aflame beneath a sky ablaze.
The streets in Capernaum are just beginning to become
crowded with women going to the fountain, fishermen
preparing their nets and boats to go fishing at night,
children running at play in the streets, little donkeys
carrying hampers heading towards the country, probably
to get vegetables.
Jesus emerges from Peter's house, at a door that opens
on to a little yard completely shaded by a vine and a
fig-tree. A stony lane runs from beyond the door, down
and along the lake.
Peter's is on the shore with Andrew, arranging the fish
baskets and nets in the boat, sorting the seats and coils
of rope, preparing for the night's fishing. Andrew, who is
helping Peter, comes and goes from the house to the
boat.
'Will you have a good haul?' Jesus asks his disciples
'The weather is right. The water is calm, it will be clear
moonlight. The fish will come to the surface from the
bottom and my net will drag them.'
'Are we going by ourselves?'
'Oh! Master! How could we manage by ourselves with this

type of net.'
'I have never gone fishing and I expect to be taught by
you. 'Jesus goes down very slowly towards the lake and
stops by the boat, on the coarse, pebbly sands.
'See, Master: this is what we do. I go out beside the boat
of James of Zebedee, and we go thus to the right point,
both boats together. Then we lower the net. We hold one
end. You said You wanted to hold it.'
'Yes, if you tell Me what I have to do.'
'Oh! You only have to watch it going down. It must be
lowered slowly without making any knots. Very slowly,
because we will be in a fishing area, and any quick
movement may drive the fish away. Without knots,
otherwise the net would close up, whereas it must open
like a bag, or if You prefer so, like a veil blown by the
wind. Then, when the net is fully lowered, we will row
gently, or we may set sail, according to circumstances,
forming a semicircle on the lake.
And when we understand by the vibration of the safety
peg that the haul is good, we head for the shore. When
we are almost on the shore – not before to avoid running
the risk of losing all the fish; not after, to avoid damaging
both the fish and net on the stones – we will haul in the
net. At this point we must be very careful, because the
boats must be so close as to allow one boat to catch the
end of the net from the other one, but they must not
collide, to avoid crushing the net full of fish. Please,
Master, be careful, it is our daily bread. Keep an eye on
the net, that jolts may not turn it over. The fish fight for
their freedom with strong strokes of their tails, and if
there is a lot of them... You will understand... They are
small things, but if ten, one hundred, a thousand get
together, they become as strong as Leviathan.'
'The same happens with sins, Peter. After all, one fault is
not irretrievable. But if one is not careful in controlling
oneself, and one adds fault to fault, at the end a little
fault, perhaps a single omission, or a simple weakness,

becomes bigger and bigger, it becomes a habit, it becomes a capital vice. At times one starts with a lustful glance and ends up by committing adultery. At times, while simply lacking charity when speaking to a relative, one ends up by doing violence to one's neighbour. Never, never allow faults to increase in gravity and in numbers, if you wish to avoid trouble! They become dangerous and overbearing like the infernal Snake himself, and they will drag you down into Gehenna.'

'What You say is right, Master... But we are so weak! '

'Care and prayer are necessary to become strong and obtain help, together with a strong will not to sin. And you must have full trust in the loving justice of the Father.'

'Do You think He will not be too severe with poor Simon?'

'He might have been severe with the old Simon. But with My Peter, with the new man, the man of His Christ... no, Peter, He will not. He loves you and will love you.'

'And what about me?'

' You, too, Andrew; and John, James, Philip and Nathanael as well. You are the first chosen by Me.'

'Will there be any more? There is Your cousin, and in Judaea... '

'Oh! There will be many more. My Kingdom is open to all mankind and I solemnly tell you that My haul, in the nights of centuries, will be more plentiful than your richest one... Because every century is one night in which not the pure light of Orion or of the sailing moon will be the guide and light of mankind, but the word of Christ and the Grace He will bestow; a night that will become the dawn of a day with no sunset and of a light in which all the faithful will live and will be the dawn of a sunshine that will make all the chosen resplendent, beautiful, happy forever even like gods. Minor gods, children of God the Father and like Me... It is not possible for you to understand now. But I solemnly tell you that your

Christian life will cause you to resemble your Master, and you will shine in Heaven with His signs. So, notwithstanding the envious malice of Satan and the weak will of men, My haul will be more plentiful than yours.'

'But shall we be Your only apostles?'

'Are you jealous, Peter? No, don't be! Others will come and in My heart there will be love for everybody. Don't be greedy, Peter. You do not yet know Who loves you. Have you ever counted the stars? Or the stones in the depth of the lake? No, you could not. And you would be even less able to count the loving throbs of which My heart is capable. Have you ever been able to count how many times this lake kisses the shore with its waves in the course of twelve moons? No, you would never be able to do so. And you would be even less able to count the loving waves that My heart pours out to kiss men. Be sure of My love, Peter.'

Peter is deeply moved and he takes Jesus' hand and kisses it.

Andrew looks, but does not dare take Jesus' hand. But Jesus caresses his hair with His hand and says: ' I love you very much, too. In the hour of your dawn, without having to lift your eyes, you will see your Jesus reflected in the vault of heaven, and He will be smiling at you to say to you: "I love you. Come", and your passing away at dawn will be sweeter than entering a nuptial chamber... '

'Simon! Simon! Andrew! Here I am... I am coming... ' calls John hurrying towards them, panting. 'Oh! Master! Have I kept You waiting?' John looks at Jesus with the eyes of a lover.

Peter answers: 'To tell you the truth, I was beginning to think you were no longer coming. Get your boat ready quickly. And James?...'

'Well... we are late because of a blind man. He thought Jesus was in our house and he came there. We said to him: "He is not here. Perhaps He will cure you tomorrow. Just wait." But he did not want to wait. James said to him: "You have been waiting so long to see the light, what does it matter if you have to wait another night?" But he will not listen to reason...'

'John, if you were blind, would you be anxious to see your mother?'

'Eh!... most certainly!'

'Well then? Where is the blind man?'

'He is coming with James. He got hold of his mantle and will not let it go. But he is coming very slowly because the shore is covered with stones, and he stumbles against them... Master, will You forgive me for being hard?'

'Yes, I will, but to make amends, go and help the blind man and bring him to Me.'

John runs away. Peter shakes his head, but says nothing. He looks at the sky which is now changing from a deep copper hue to blue. He looks at the lake and at the other boats that are already out fishing and he sighs.

'Simon?'

'Master?'

'Don't be afraid. You will have a good haul, even if you are the last one to go out.'

'Also this time?'

'Every time you are charitable, God will grant you the grace of abundance.'

'Here is the blind man.'

The poor blind man approaches between James and John, carrying a walking stick in his hand, but at present, he does not use it and he walks better supported by the two young men.

'Here, man, the Master is in front of you.'

The blind man kneels down: 'My Lord! Have mercy on me.'

'Do you want to see? Stand up. How long have you been blind?'

The four apostles gather round the other two.

'Seven years, Lord. Before, I could see well, and I worked. I was a blacksmith at Caesarea on-the- Sea. I was doing well. The harbour, the good trading, they always needed me for one job or another. But whilst striking a piece of iron to make an anchor-and You can imagine how red hot it was to be pliable- a splinter came off it, and burnt my eye. My eyes were already sore from the heat of the forge. I lost the wounded eye, and also the other one became blind after three months. I have finished all my savings, and now I live on charity...'

'Are you alone?'

'I am married with three little children... ; I have not even seen the face of one of them... and I have an old mother. And yet she and my wife earn a little bread, and with what they earn and the alms I take home, we manage not to starve. If I were cured!... I would go back to work. All I ask for is to be able to work like a good Israelite and thus feed those I love.'

'And you came to Me? Who told you?'

'A leper who was cured by You at the foot of Mount Tabor, when You were coming back to the lake after that beautiful speech of Yours.'

'What did he tell you?'

'That You can do everything. That You are the health of bodies and of souls. That You are a light for souls and bodies, because You are the Light of God. He, although a leper, had dared to mingle with the crowd, at the risk of being stoned, all enveloped in his mantle, because he had seen You passing by on the way to the mountain, and Your face had kindled hope in his heart. He said to me: "I saw something in that face that whispered to me: ‹There is health there. Go!› And I went." Then he repeated Your speech to me and he told me that You cured him, touching him with Your hand, without any disgust. He was coming back from the priest after his purification. I knew him. I had done some work for him when he had a store at Caesarea. I came, asking for You in every town and village. Now I have found You... Have mercy on me!'

'Come. The light is still too bright for one coming out of darkness!'

'Are you going to cure me, then?'

Jesus takes him to Peter's house and in the dim light of the kitchen garden, He places the blind man before Him such that the cured eyes may not see the , as first sight, the lake still sparkling with light. Like a very docile child, the man obeys without questions.

Jesus stretches His hands over the head of the kneeling man and prays:

'Father! Your Light to this son of Yours!'

He remains in this position for a moment. Then He wets His fingers-tips with saliva and then lightly touches lightly the open, but lifeless eyes with His right hand.

A moment. Then the man blinks, rubs his eyelids as one awakening from sleep.

'What do you see?'

'Oh!... oh!... oh!... Eternal God! I think... I think... oh! That I can see... I see Your mantle... it's red, isn't it? And a white hand... and a woollen belt... oh! Good Jesus... I can see better and better, the more I get used to seeing... There is the grass of the earth... and that is certainly a well... and there is a vine... '

'Stand up, My friend.'

The man stands up, crying and laughing at once. For a moment, he hesitates, torn between respect and desire and then he raises his face and meets Jesus' eyes. Jesus is smiling, full of merciful love. How beautiful it must be to recover one's sight and to see that face as the first one! Instinctively, the man shouts and stretches but then controls himself. But Jesus opens His arms and draws to Himself the man who is much smaller than He. 'Go home now, and be happy and just. Go with My peace.'

'Master, Master! Lord! Jesus! Holy! Blessed! The light...

I see... I see everything... There is the blue lake, the clear sky, the setting sun, and then the horns of the waxing moon... But it is in Your eyes that I see the most beautiful and clear blue, and in You I see the beauty of the most real sun, and the chaste light of the blessed moon. You are the Star of those who suffer, the Light of the blind, the living active Mercy!'

'I am the Light of souls. Be a son of the Light.'

'Yes, Jesus, always. Every time I close my re-born eyes, I will renew my oath. May You and the Most High be blessed.'

'Blessed be the Most High Father! Go!'

And the man goes away, happy, sure of himself, while Jesus and the dumbfounded apostles get into two boats and manoeuvre away.

Jesus Prays At Night

It is the dead of night and the starry canopy of the sky is faintly reflected in the glitter of lake Galilee, which itself, though not visible in the dark, one guesses that it is there peacefully sleeping under the stars because of the gentle lapping of its waters on the gravel shore.

Without making a noise, Jesus comes out of Peter's house in Capernaum, where he has spent the night to make Peter happy. Setting the door ajar, Jesus looks thoughtfully up at the sky, the lake and the road and then begins walking towards the village, away from the lake. He passes through part of it heading towards the country and along a little path that leads to the first undulations of an olive-grove, where He enters the green, silent peace and prostrates Himself in prayer. Fervently, He prays, kneeling down and sighing perhaps because of some moral grief, and then, as if fortified, He rises, standing straight up, His face raised to Heaven, a face made more spiritual by the rising light of a clear summer dawn. With His arms fully outstretched, He seems a tall living angelical cross. He prays now, smiling. So gentle in His attitude, He seems to be blessing the whole country, the rising day, the fading stars and the lake now becoming more visible with the dawning light.

'Master! We have been looking for You all over! We saw
the door ajar, when we came back with the fish, and we
thought You had gone out. But we could not find You.
And at last, a peasant, who was loading his baskets
to take them to town, told us. We were calling: "Jesus,
Jesus!", and he said: "Are you looking for the Rabbi Who
speaks to the crowds? He went up that path, up towards
the mountain. He must be in Micah's olive-grove, because
He often goes there. I have seen Him there before." He
was right. Why did You come out so early, Master? Why
did You not rest? Was the bed not comfortable? ... '
'No, Peter. The bed was comfortable and the room was
lovely. But I often do that. To raise My spirit and be
united to the Father. Prayer is a strength for oneself and
for others. We achieve everything by praying. If we do not
receive a grace, which the Father does not always grant
– and we must not think it is due to lack of love, instead
we must believe that it is the will of an Order which
governs the destiny of every man for a good purpose
prayer certainly gives us peace and contentment, to
enable us to bear so many vexing things, without going
off the holy path. It is easy, you know, Peter, to have a
clouded mind and an agitated heart because of what is
around us! And how can a clouded mind or an agitated
heart perceive God? '
'It's true. But we do not know how to pray! We are not
capable of saying the lovely words You say. '
'Say the words you know, as best as you can. It is not the
words, but the sentiments with which they are uttered
that make your prayers pleasant to the Father. '
'We would like to pray as You do.'
'I will teach you also to pray. I will teach you the most
holy prayer. But to prevent it from being only a void
formula on your lips, I want your hearts to have at least
a minimum of holiness, light and wisdom... That is why I
instruct you. Later, I will teach you the holy prayer. Why
were you looking for Me, is there anything you want of

Me? '

'No, Master. But there are many who want so much from You. There were already people coming from Capernaum, and they were poor, sick, depressed people, people of good will and anxious to be taught. When they inquired about You, we said: "The Master is tired and is sleeping. Go away and come back next Sabbath."'

'No, Simon. You must not say that. There is not one day only for mercy. I am Love, Light and Health every day of the week. '

'But... so far You have spoken only on Sabbaths.'

'Because I was still unknown. But as I become known, every day there will be effusions of Grace and graces. I tell you solemnly that the time will come when even the moment of time which is granted to a sparrow to rest on a branch and eat some little grains will not be granted to the Son of man for His rest and meals. '

'But You will be taken ill! We will not allow that. Your kindness must not make You unhappy.'

'And do you think that could make Me unhappy? Oh! If all the world came to Me to listen to Me, to bewail its sins and sorrow on My heart, to be healed in its bodies and souls, and I were worn out speaking, and forgiving and pouring forth My power, I would be so happy, Peter, that I would not even regret Heaven, where I was in the Father! Where were they from, those who were coming to Me? '

'From Korazim, Bethsaida, Capernaum, and there were some even from Tiberias and Gherghesa, as well as from the hundreds of villages around those towns. '

'Go and tell them that I will be at Korazim, Bethsaida and nearby villages. '

'Why not at Capernaum? '

'Because I came for everybody and everybody must have Me, and then... there is old Isaac waiting for Me. We must not disappoint his hopes. '

'Will You wait for us here, then? '

'No, I am going and you will stay at Capernaum to send

the crowds to Me; I will come back later. '
'We will be here alone... 'Peter is sad.
'Do not be sad. Obedience should make you happy as
well as the conviction that you are a useful disciple. And
the same applies to the others.'
Peter, Andrew, James and John cheer up. Jesus blesses
them, and they part.

The Miraculous Draught Of Fishes

'When all the trees bloom in spring, the happy farmer
says: "I will have a good crop" and that hope causes his
heart to rejoice.... ' Says Jesus, speaking to the crowd.
'...But from springtime to autumn, from the month of
flowers to the month of fruit, how many days, winds,
rains, sunshine and storms must pass, and sometimes
wars or the cruelty of the mighty ones and diseases of
plants, and at times diseases of the men of the fields, so
that the plants, no longer hoed up, no longer watered,
pruned, supported or cleaned, although they promised
copious fruit, wilt and die or bear no fruit!
You follow Me. You love Me. Like plants in springtime
you adorn yourselves with purpose and love. Israel,
indeed, at the dawn of My mission is like our sweet
countryside in the bright month of Nisan. But listen. Like
the excessive heat in dry weather, Satan, who is envious
of Me, will come to scorch you with his wrath. The world
will come with its icy winds to freeze your blooms. And
passions will come like storms. And tedium will come
like a persistent rain. All My enemies and yours will
come to sterilise what should be the fruit of your natural
tendency to bloom in God.
I am warning you, because I know. Will everything then
be lost, when I, like a sick farmer, even more than sick:
dead, will no longer be able to speak to you and work

miracles for you? No. I will sow and cultivate as long as I
have time. Then everything will grow and ripen for you, if
you keep a good watch.
Look at the fig-tree near the house of Simon of Jonas.
Who planted it did not find the right and most favourable
spot. Planted as it was near the damp northern wall,
it would have withered, if by itself it had not found
protection to survive. And it sought sunshine and light.
There it is: all bent, but strong and proud, drawing in
the rays of the sun from early dawn and converting
them into nourishment for its hundreds and hundreds
of sweet fruits. It defended itself by itself. It said: "The
Creator wanted me, that I may give joy and food to man.
And I want to join my will to His." A fig-tree! A speechless
tree! A soulless tree! And will you, children of God, the
children of man, will you be inferior to a wooden plant?
Keep a good watch to bear fruits of eternal life. I will
cultivate You, and at the end I will give you such a potent
juice, that you will never find a more powerful one. Do
not allow Satan to laugh at the destruction of My work, of
My sacrifice and of your souls. Seek light. Seek sunshine.
Seek strength. Seek life. I am the Life, Strength,
Sunshine and Light of those who love Me. I have come to
take you whence I came. I am speaking to you here, to
call You all and point out to you the ten commandments
that give eternal life. And with loving advice I say to you:
"Love God and your neighbour." It is the first condition to
fulfil everything else well. It is the most holy of the holy
commandments. Love. Those who love God, in God and
for the Lord God, will have peace both on the earth and
in Heaven, for their abode and their crown. '
People go away with difficulty after Jesus' blessing. There
are neither sick nor poor people.
Jesus says to Simon: 'Call the other two. Let us go on to
the lake and cast the net. '
'Master, my arms ache with fatigue: all night I cast and
hauled the net, and all in vain. The fish are down at the

bottom. I wonder where.'
'Do as I tell you, Peter. Always listen to those who love you.'
'I will do as You say, out of respect for Your word.' And he shouts to the assistants and also to James and John: 'Let us go out fishing. The Master wants to go. 'And as they set off, he says to Jesus: 'However, Master, I assure You that it is not the right time. Goodness knows where the fish will be resting just now!... '

Jesus, sitting at the prow, smiles and is silent.
They form a semicircle on the lake and then cast the net. After a few minutes' waiting, the boat is shaken in a strange way, because the lake is as smooth as a glass pane under the midday sun.
'But that is fish, Master! ' says Peter, with his eyes wide open. Jesus smiles and is silent.
'Heave ho! Heave ho! ' Peter' orders his assistants. But the boat lists to one side, where the net is: 'Hey there! James! John! Quick! Come Quick! With the oars! Quick! '
They rush and the joint efforts of the two crews succeed in hauling in the net without damaging the catch. The two boats draw closer until they are united and one, two, ...five, ...ten baskets all full of wonderful fish, and there are still so many wriggling in the net: live silver and bronze, struggling to escape death. There is only one thing to be done: to empty the net into the bottom of the boats.

They do that and the bottoms become a turmoil of agonizing lives. And the crew are up to their ankles in such abundance that the boats sink below the water-line because of the excessive weight.
'To the shore! Steer! Quick! The sails! Watch the depth line! Have the poles ready to prevent a clash. We have too much weight! '
As long as the manoeuvre lasts, Peter thinks of nothing

else. But when he gets ashore, he begins to realise. He understands. He is frightened. 'Master! My Lord! Go away from me! I am a sinner! I am not worthy of being near You! ' He is on his knees on the damp shore.

Jesus looks at him and smiles: 'Get up! Follow Me! I will not leave you anymore! From now on, you will be a fisher of men, and your companions with you. Be afraid of nothing. I am calling you. Come! '

'At once, Lord. You look after the boats. Take everything to Zebedee and to my brother-in-law. Let us go. We are all for You, Jesus! Blessed be the Eternal Father for this choice. '

The Iscariot Finds Jesus At Gethsemane And Is Accepted As A Disciple

It is evening, turning dark and the daylight grows fainter and fainter in the thick olive-grove where, Jesus, alone, is sitting on one of the little ground terraces, in His familiar posture; His elbows resting on His knees, His forearms forward and His hands joined. He has taken off His mantle as though He were warm, and His white tunic stands out against the green of the surroundings made even darker by the twilight.

A man approaches through the olive-trees and seems to be looking for something or someone. He is tall, and his garments gay: of a yellow pink hue that makes his big mantle more flamboyant, adorned as it is with swinging fringes. His face is somewhat obscured by the dim light and the distance, and also because the edge of his mantle falls over part of his face. When he sees Jesus, he makes a gesture as if to say: 'There He is! 'And he hastens his step. When he is a few meters away, he greets Him: 'Hail, Master! '

Jesus turns round suddenly and looks up, because the man is standing on the next terrace, which is higher up. Jesus looks at him, His expression serious and also sad. The man says again: 'I greet You, Master. I am Judas of Kerioth. Do You not recognize me? Do You not

remember? '

'I remember and recognize you. You spoke to Me here with Thomas, last Passover.'

'And You said to me: "Think about it and make up your mind before I come back." I have made up my mind. I will come. '

'Why are you coming, Judas? 'Jesus is really sad.

'Because... The last time I told You why. Because I dream of the Kingdom of Israel and I see You as a king. '

'Is that why you are coming? '

'Yes, it is. I will put myself and everything I possess: capability, acquaintances, friends, and fatigue at Your service and at the service of Your mission to rebuild Israel. '

The two, now close, standing face to face, stare at each other; Jesus is grave and melancholy. Judas, exalted by his dream, is smiling, handsome, young, sprightly and ambitious.

'I did not look for you, Judas. '

'I know. But I looked for You. For days and days I have been putting people at the gates to warn me of Your arrival. I thought You would be coming with followers and would therefore be easy to notice. Instead... I understood that You had been here, because a group of pilgrims was blessing You because You had cured a sick man. But no one could tell me where You were. Then I remembered this place. And I have come. If I had not found You here, I would have resigned myself to not finding You any more... '

'Do you think it is a good thing for you, that you found
Me? '

'Yes, because I was looking for You. I was longing for You,
I want You. '

'Why? Why did you look for Me? '

'But I have told You, Master! Did You not understand? '

'I did understand you. Yes, I did. But I want you also to
understand Me before you follow Me. Come. We will walk
and talk. 'And they start walking, one beside the other,
up and down the paths that criss-cross in the olive-
grove. 'You want to follow Me for a human reason, Judas.
But I must dissuade you. I have not come for that.'

'But are You not the designated King of the Jews? The
one of whom the Prophets spoke? Others have come. But
they lacked too many things and they fell like leaves no
longer supported by the wind. But You have God with
You, in fact You work miracles. Where there is God, the
success of the mission is guaranteed. '

'You have spoken the truth. I have God with Me. I am
His Word. I was prophesied by the Prophets, promised to
the Patriarchs, expected by the people. But why, Israel,
have you become so blind and deaf that you are no
longer able to read and see, to hear and understand the
reality of events? My Kingdom is not of this world, Judas.
Allow yourself to be convinced of that. I have come to
Israel to bring Light and Glory. But not the light and
glory of the earth. I have come to call the just of Israel to
the Kingdom. Because it is from Israel that the plant of
eternal life is to come, and with Israel it is to be formed,
the plant, the sap of which will be the Blood of the Lord,
the plant that will spread all over the earth, until the
end of time. My first followers will be from Israel. My first

confessors will be from Israel. But also My persecutors will be from Israel. Also My executioners will be from Israel. And also My traitor will Be from Israel... '

'No, Master. That will never happen. If everyone should betray You, I will remain with You and defend You.'

'You, Judas? And on what do you base your certainty?'

'On my honour as a man.'

'Which is more fragile than a cobweb, Judas. It is God we have to ask for the strength to be honest and faithful. Man!... Man accomplishes human deeds. To accomplish spiritual deeds – and to follow the Messiah with truthfulness and justice is to accomplish a spiritual deed – it is necessary to kill man and make him be born again. Are you capable of so much?'

'Yes, Master. And in any case... Not everybody in Israel will love You. But Israel will not give the Messiah executioners and traitors. Israel has been waiting for You for centuries! '

'I will be given them. Remember the Prophets... Their words... and their end. I am destined to disappoint many. And you are one of them. Judas, you have here in front of you a mild, peaceful poor man, who wishes to remain poor. I have not come to impose Myself and make war. I am not going to contend with the strong and mighty ones for any kingdom or any power. I contend only with Satan for souls and I have come to break the chains of Satan with the fire of My love. I have come to teach mercy, sacrifice, humility, continence. I say to you and to everybody: "Do not crave for human wealth, but work for eternal coins." You are deceiving yourself if you think I am to triumph over Rome and the ruling classes. Herods and Caesars can sleep tranquilly, while I speak to the

crowds. I have not come to snatch anybody's sceptre...
and My eternal sceptre is already ready, but no one,
unless one was love as I am, would like to hold it. Go,
Judas, and ponder... '

'Are You rejecting me, Master?'

'I reject nobody, because who rejects does not love. But,
tell Me, Judas: how would you describe the gesture of
a man, who, knowing he is infected by a contagious
disease, says to another man who approaches him
unaware of the situation, to drink out of his chalice:
"Watch what you are doing"? Would you define it hatred
or love?'

'I would say it was love, because he does not want the
man, unaware of the danger, to ruin his health.'

'Well, define also My gesture likewise.'

'Can I ruin my health coming with You? No, never.'

'You can ruin more than your health, because, consider
this carefully, Judas, little will be debited to him who
is a murderer, but believes he is doing justice, and he
believes it because he does not know the Truth; but a
great deal will be debited to him, who knowing the Truth,
not only does not follow it, but becomes its enemy.'

'I will not do that. Take me, Master. You cannot refuse
me. If You are the Saviour and You see that I am a
sinner, a sheep astray, a blind man off the right path,
why do You refuse to save me? Take me. I will follow You,
even to death... '

'To death! That is true. Then...'

'Then, Master?'

'The future is in God's bosom. Go. We will meet tomorrow at the Fish Gate.'

'Thank You, Master. The Lord be with You.'

'And may His mercy save you.'

Jesus With Judas Iscariot Meets Simon Zealot And John

'Are You sure he will come? 'Asks Judas Iscariot as he walks up and down with Jesus near one of the gates within the Temple enclosure.

'I am certain. He was leaving Bethany at dawn and at Gethsemane he was to meet My first disciple... '

There is a pause. Then Jesus stops in front of Judas and stares at him, studying him closely. Then He places a hand on Judas' shoulder and asks: ' Why, Judas, do you not tell Me your thoughts? '

'What thoughts? I have no special thought, Master, at the present moment. I ask You even too many questions. You certainly cannot complain of my muteness. '

'You ask Me many questions and You give Me many details on the town and its inhabitants. But you do not unburden yourself to Me. What do you think it matters to Me, what you tell Me about the wealth of people and the members of this or that family? I am not an idler who has come here to while away the time. You know why I have come. And you may well realize that I am concerned with being the Master of My disciples, as the most important thing. I therefore want sincerity and trust from them. Was your father fond of you, Judas? '

'He was very fond of me. He was proud of me. When I went back home from school, and even later, when I went back to Kerioth from Jerusalem, he wanted me to tell him everything. He took an interest in everything I did and he would rejoice if they were good things, he would comfort me if they were not so good, if sometimes, You know, we all make mistakes – if I had made a mistake and had been blamed for it, he would show me the fairness of the reproach I had received, or the injustice of my action. But he did it so gently... he seemed an older brother. He always ended by saying: "I am saying this because I want my Judas to be just. I want to be blessed through my son." My father... '

Jesus, Who has carefully observed how moved Judas is at the recall of the memories of his father, says: 'Now, Judas, be sure of what I am going to tell you. Nothing will make your father so happy, as your being a faithful disciple. Your father, who brought you up as you said, must have been a just man and his soul will rejoice, where he is awaiting the light, seeing that you are My disciple. But in order to be such, you must say to yourself: "I have found my lost father, the father who was like an older brother to me, I have found him in my Jesus, and I will tell Him everything, as I used to tell my beloved father, over whose death I am still mourning, that I may receive from Him guidance, blessings or a kind reproach." May God grant it, and above all may you behave so that Jesus will always say to you: "You are good. I bless you." '

'Oh! Yes, Jesus! If You love me so much, I will strive to be good, as You want and my father wanted me to be. And my mother will no longer have an aching pain in her heart. She used to say: "You have no guide now, my son, and you still need one so much." When she knows that I have You! '

'I will love you as no other man could possibly love you, I will love you so much, I do love you. Do not disappoint Me. '

'No, Master, I will not. I was full of conflicts. Envy, jealousy, eagerness to excel, sensuality, everything clashed in me against the voice of my conscience. Even quite recently, see? You caused me to suffer. That is: no, not You. It was my wicked nature... I thought I was Your first disciple... and, now You have just told me that You already have one. '

'You saw him yourself. Do you not remember that at Passover I was in the Temple with many Galileans? '

'I thought they were friends... I thought I was the first one to be chosen for such destiny, and that I was therefore the dearest. '

'There are no distinctions in My heart between the first and the last. If the first one should err and the last one were a holy man, then there would be a distinction in the eyes of God. But I will love just the same: I will love the holy living man with a blissful love, and the sinner with a suffering love. But here is John coming with Simon. John, My first disciple, Simon, the one of whom I spoke to you two days ago. You have already seen Simon and John. One was ill...'

'Ah! The leper! I remember. Is he already Your disciple? '

'Since the following day. '

'And why did I have to wait so long? '

'Judas?! '

'You are right. Forgive me. '

John sees the Master, points Him out to Simon and they make haste.

John and the Master kiss each other. Simon, instead, throws himself at Jesus' feet and kisses them, exclaiming: 'Glory to my Saviour! Bless Your servant that his actions may be holy in the eyes of God and that I may glorify Him and bless Him for giving You to me. '

Jesus places His hand on Simon's head: 'Yes, I bless you to thank you for your work. Get up, Simon. This is John, and this is Simon: here is My last disciple. He also wants to follow the Truth. He is therefore a brother to you all. '

They greet each other: the two Judaeans inquisitively, John heartily.

'Are you tired, Simon? 'asks Jesus.

'No, Master. With my health I have recovered a vitality I never felt before. '

'And I know you make good use of it. I have spoken to many people and they all told Me that you have already instructed them about the Messiah. '

Simon smiles happily. 'Also last night I spoke of You to one who is an honest Israelite. I hope You will meet him one day. I would like to take You to him. '

'That is quite possible. '

Judas joins in the conversation: 'Master, You promised to come with me, in Judaea. '

'And I will. Simon will continue to teach the people on My coming. The time is short, My dear friends, and the people are so many. I will now go with Simon. You two will come and meet Me this evening on the road to the

Mount of Olives and we will give money to the poor. Go now. '

When Jesus is alone with Simon, He asks him: 'Is that person in Bethany a true Israelite? '

'He is a true Israelite. His ideas are the prevailing ones, but he is really longing for the Messiah. And when I said to him: "He is now among us", he replied at once: "I am blessed because I am living this hour." '

'We shall go to him one day and take our blessing to his house. Have you seen the new disciple? '

'I have. He is young and seems intelligent.'

'Yes, he is. Since you are a Judaean, You will bear more with him than the others will, because of his ideas. '

'Is that a desire, or an order? '

'A kind order. You have suffered and You can be more indulgent. Sorrow teaches many things. '

'If You give me an order, I will be totally indulgent to him. '

'Yes. Be so. Perhaps Peter, and he may not be the only one, will be somewhat upset seeing how I take care and worry about this disciple. But one day, they will understand... The more one is deformed, the more assistance one needs.

The others... oh! The others form properly, also by themselves, by simple contact. I do not want to do everything by Myself. I want the will of man and the help of other people to form a man. I ask you to help Me... and I am grateful for the help. '

'Master do You think he will disappoint You? '

'No. But he is young and was brought up in Jerusalem. '

'Oh! near You he will amend all the vices of that town... I am sure. I was already old and hardened by bitter hatred, and yet I have changed completely after seeing You... '

Jesus whispers: 'So be it! 'Then in a loud voice: 'Let us go to the Temple. I will evangelize the people. '

END

Jesus with Judas Iscariot Meets Simon Zealot and John.

Extracts from the Next in Series

For Love That Perseveres

It is time to say goodbye and Jesus and His disciples
are standing at the door of a poor hut, with Jonah and
other poor peasants, lit by a light so faint, it seems to be
blinking.

'Will I not see You again, my Lord? ' asks Jonah.

'You have brought light to our hearts. Your kindness has
turned these days into a feast that will last all our lives.
But You have seen how we are treated. A mule is taken
better care of than we are. And trees receive more human
attention; they are money. We are only millstones that
earn money and we are used until we die of excessive
toil. But Your words have been as many loving caresses.
Our bread seemed more plentiful and it tasted better
because You shared it with us; this bread which he does
not even give to his dogs. Come back to share it with us,
my Lord. Only because it is You, I dare say that. It would
be an insult to offer anyone else shelter and food which
even a beggar would disdain. But You...'

'But I find in them a heavenly perfume and flavour
because in them there is faith and love. I will come,
Jonah. I will come back. You stay in your place, tied
like an animal to the shafts. May your place be Jacob's
ladder. And in fact angels go and come from Heaven
down to you, carefully gathering all your merits and
taking them up to God. But I will come to you. To relieve
your spirit. Be faithful to Me, all of you. Oh! I would like
to give you also human peace. But I cannot. I must say
to you: go on suffering. And that is very sad for One Who
loves...'

'Lord, if You love us, we no longer suffer. Before we had no one to love us...Oh! If I could, at least, see Your Mother! '

'Do not worry. I will bring Her to you. When the weather is milder, I will come with Her. Do not risk incurring cruel punishments on account of your anxiety to see Her. You must wait for Her as you wait for the rising of a star, of the evening star. She will appear to you all of a sudden, exactly as the evening star, which is not there one moment, and a moment later it shines in the sky. And you must consider that even now She is lavishing Her gifts of love on you. Goodbye, everybody. May My peace protect you from the harshness of him who torments you. Goodbye, Jonah. Do not cry. You have waited for so many years with patient faith. I now promise you a very short wait. Do not weep; I will not leave you alone. Your kindness wiped My tears when I was a New-Born Baby. Is Mine not sufficient to wipe yours?'

'Yes... but You are going away... and I have to remain here...'

'Jonah, My friend, do not make Me go away depressed because I cannot comfort you ...'

'I am not crying, my Lord... But how will I be able to live without seeing You, now that I know that You are alive?'

Jesus caresses the forlorn old man once again and then goes away. But standing on the edge of the miserable threshing floor, Jesus stretches His arms out and blesses the country. Then He departs.

'What have You done, Master?' asks Simon who has noticed the unusual gesture...

'I put a seal on everything. That no demon may damage things and thus cause trouble to those wretched people. I could do no more...'

'Master, let us walk on a little faster. I would like to tell You something which I do not want the others to hear.

'They move farther away from the group and Simon begins to speak:

'I wanted to tell You that Lazarus has instructions to use my money to assist all those who apply to him in Jesus' name. Could we not free Jonah? That man is worn out and his only joy is to be with You. Let us give him that. What is his work worth here? If instead he were free, he would be Your disciple in this beautiful yet desolate plain. The richest people in Israel own fertile estates here and they exploit them with cruel extortion, exacting a hundredfold profit from their workers. I have known that for years. You will not be able to stop here long, because the sect of the Pharisees rules over the country and I do not think it will ever be friendly to You. These oppressed and hopeless workers are the most unhappy people in Israel. Your heard it Yourself, not even at Passover have they peace, neither can they pray, whilst their severe masters, with solemn gestures and affected exhibitions, take up prominent positions in front of all the people. At least they will have the joy of knowing that You exist and of listening to Your words repeated to them by one who will not alter one single letter. If You agree Master, please say so, and Lazarus will do what is necessary.'

'Simon, I knew why you gave all your property away. The thoughts of men are known to Me. And I loved you also because of that. By making Jonah happy, you make Jesus happy. Oh! How it torments Me to see good people suffer! My situation of a poor man despised by the world afflicts Me only because of that. If Judas heard Me, he would say: "But are You not the Word of God? Give the order and these stones will become gold and bread for the poor people." He would repeat Satan's snare. I am anxious to satisfy people's hunger. But not the way Judas would like. You are not yet sufficiently mature to grasp the depth of what I want to say. But I will tell you: if God saw to everything He would rob His friends. He would deprive them of the chance of being merciful and fulfilling the commandment of love. My friends must possess this mark of God in common with Him: the holy mercy consisting in deeds and words. And the unhappiness of other people gives My friends the opportunity to practice it. Have you understood what I mean?'

'Your thought is a deep one. I will ponder Your words. And I humble myself as I see how dull-minded I am and how great God is Who wants us to be gifted with all His most sweet attributes so that He may call us His children. God is revealed to me in His manifold perfections by every ray of light with which You illuminate my heart. Day by day, like one advancing in an unknown place, the knowledge of the immense Thing which is the Perfection Which wants to call us His "children" progresses in me and I seem to climb like an eagle or to dive like a fish into two endless depths like sky and sea, and I climb higher and higher and dive deeper and deeper but I never touch the end. But what is, therefore, God?'

'God is the unattainable Perfection, God is the perfect Beauty, God is the infinite Power, God is the incomprehensible Essence, God is the unsurpassable Bounty, God is the indestructible Mercy, God is the immeasurable Wisdom, God is the Love that became God. He is the Love! He is the Love! You say that the more you know God in His perfection, the higher you seem to climb and the deeper to dive into two endless depths of shadeless blue... But when you understand what is the Love that became God, you will no longer climb or dive into the blue but into a blazing vortex and you will be drawn towards a beatitude that will be death and life for you. You will possess God, with a perfect possession,

when, by your will, you succeed in understanding and deserving Him. You will then be fixed in His perfection.'
'O Lord... ' exhales Simon, overwhelmed. They walk in silence until they reach the road where Jesus stops to wait for the others. When they regroup again, Levi kneels down: 'I should be leaving, Master. But Your servant asks You a favour. Take me to Your Mother. This man is an orphan like me. Do not deny me what You give him, that I may see the face of a mother...'
'Come. What is asked in My Mother's name, I grant in My Mother's name.'

The sun, although about to set, blazes down unto the grey- green dome of the thick olive trees laden with small well- shaped fruit but only penetrates the tangle of branches enough to provide a few tiny eyelets of light whereas the main road, on the other hand, embedded between two banks, is a dusty blazing dazzling ribbon. Alone and walking fast among the olive trees, Jesus smiles to Himself... He smiles even more happily when He reaches a cliff... Nazareth....its panorama flickering in the heat of the blazing sun...and Jesus begins to descend and quickens His step. Now on the silent, deserted road, He has protected His head with His mantle and, no longer minding the sun, is walking so fast that the mantle is blowing at His sides and behind Him so that He seems to be flying. Now and again, the voice of a child or of a woman from inside a house or a kitchen garden reaches Jesus where He is walking in the shady spots provided by garden trees whose branches extend into the road. He turns into a half shaded road where there are women gathered around a cool well and they all salute Him, welcoming Him in shrill voices.
'Peace to you all... But please be silent. I want to give My Mother a surprise.'

'Her sister-in-law has just gone away with a pitcher
of cool water. But she is coming back. They are left
without any water. The spring is either dry or the water
is absorbed by the parched land before reaching Your
garden. We don't know. That's what Mary of Alphaeus
was saying. There she is... she is coming.'

Not having seen Jesus yet, the mother of Judas and
James, with an amphora on her head and another in her
hand, is shouting; 'I'll be quicker this way. Mary is very
sad, because Her flowers are dying of thirst. They are
the ones planted by Joseph and Jesus and it breaks Her
heart to see them withering.'
'But now that She sees Me... ' says Jesus appearing from
behind the group of women.
'Oh! My Jesus! Blessed You are! I'll go and tell...'
'No. I will go. Give Me the amphoras.'
The door is half shut. Mary is in the garden. Oh!
How happy She will be! She was speaking of You also
this morning. But why come in this heat! You are all
perspiration! Are You alone?'
'No. With friends. But I came ahead of them to see My
Mother first. And Judas?'
'He is at Capernaum. He often goes there.' says Mary.
And she smiles as she dries Jesus' wet face with her
veil. The pitchers now ready, Jesus takes two, tying
one at each end of His belt which He throws across His
shoulder and then takes a third one in His hand. Then
He walks away, turns round a corner, reaches the house,
pushes the door, enters the little room that seems dark in
comparison with the bright sunshine outside. Slowly, He
lifts the curtain at the garden door and He watches. Mary
is standing near a rose-bush with Her back to the house,
pitying the parched plant. Jesus lays the pitcher on the
floor and the copper tinkles against a stone.

'Are you here already, Mary?' says His Mother without turning round. 'Come, come, look at this rose! And these poor lilies. They will all die if we do not assist them. Bring also some small canes to hold up this falling stalk.'
'I will bring You everything, Mother.'

Mary springs round and for a moment, She remains with Her eyes wide open then with a cry She runs with outstretched arms towards Her Son, Who has already opened His arms and is waiting for Her with the most loving smile.
'Oh! My Son!'
'Mother! Dear!' Their embrace is a long and loving one and Mary is so happy that She does not feel how hot Jesus is. But then She notices it:
'Why, Son, did You come at this time of the day? You are purple red and perspiring like a sodden sponge. Come inside. That I may dry and refresh You. I will bring You a fresh tunic and clean sandals. My Son! My Son! Why go about in this heat! The plants are dying because of the heat and You, My Flower, are going about.'
'It was to come to You as soon as possible, Mother.'
'Oh! My dear! Are You thirsty? You must be. I will now prepare...'
'Yes, I am thirsty for Your kisses, Mother. And for Your caresses. Let Me stay like this, with My head on Your shoulder, as when I was a little boy... Oh! Mother! How I miss You!'
'Tell Me to come, Son, and I will. What did You lack because of My absence? The food You like? Clean clothes? A well-made bed? Oh! My Joy, tell Me what You lacked. Your servant, My Lord, will endeavour to provide.'
'Nothing, but You...' Hand in hand, Mother and Son go into the house. Jesus sits on the chest near the wall, embraces Mary Who is in front of Him, resting His head

on Her heart and kissing Her now and again. Now He
stares at Her: 'Let Me look at You to My heart's content,
holy Mother of Mine.'
'Your tunic first. It is not good for You to remain so
damp. Come.' Jesus obeys. When He comes back
wearing a fresh looking tunic, they resume their sweet
conversation.
'I have come with My disciples and friends but I left them
in Melcha's wood. They will come tomorrow at dawn. I... I
could not wait any longer. My Mother!... ' and He kisses
Her hands.'
Mary of Alphaeus has gone away to leave us alone.
She also understood how anxious I was to be with You.
Tomorrow...tomorrow You will attend to My friends and
I to the Nazarenes. But this evening You are My Friend
and I am Yours. I brought You... Oh! Mother: I found the
shepherds of Bethlehem. And I brought You two of them:
they are orphans and You are the Mother of all men. And
more so of orphans. And I brought You also one who
needs You to control himself. And another one who is a
just man and has suffered so much. And then John...
And I brought You the recollections of Elias, Isaac,
Tobias, now called Matthew, John and Simeon. Jonah
is the most unhappy of them all. I will take You to him...
I promised him. I will continue to look for the others.
Samuel and Joseph are resting in the peace of God.'
'Were You at Bethlehem?'
'Yes, Mother. I took there the disciples who were with Me.
And I brought You these little flowers, that were growing
near the stones of the threshold.'
'Oh! ' Mary takes the withered stems and kisses them.
'And what about Anne?'
'She died in Herod's slaughter.'
'Oh! Poor woman! She was so fond of You!'
'The Bethlehemites suffered a lot. But they have not been

fair to the shepherds. But they suffered a lot...'
'But they were good to You then!'
'Yes. And that is why they are to be pitied. Satan
is jealous of their past kindness and urges them to
evil things. I was also at Hebron. The shepherds,
persecuted...'
'Oh! To that extent?!'
'Yes, they were helped by Zacharias, who got them jobs
and food, even if their masters were hard people. But
they are just souls and they turned their persecutions
and wounds into merits of true holiness. I gathered them
together. I cured Isaac... and I gave My name to a little
boy... At Juttah, where Isaac was languishing and where
he came back to life again, there is now an innocent
group, called Mary, Joseph and Jesai...'
'Oh! Your Name!'
'And Yours and the name of the Just One. And at
Kerioth, the fatherland of a disciple, a faithful Israelite
died resting on My heart. Out of joy, having found Me...
And then... Ah! how many things I have to tell You, My
perfect Friend, sweet Mother! But first of all, I beg You,
I ask You to have so much mercy on those who will be
coming tomorrow. Listen: they love Me... but they are
not perfect. You, Teacher of virtue... oh! Mother, help
Me to make them good... I would like to save them all... '
Jesus has slipped at Mary's feet. She now appears in Her
Motherly majesty.
'My Son! What do You want Your poor Mother to do better
than You do?'
'To sanctify them... Your virtue sanctifies. I brought them
here deliberately, Mother... one day I will say to You:
"Come", because it will then be urgent to sanctify souls,
that I may find them willing to be redeemed. And I will
not be able by Myself... Your silence will be as eloquent
as My words. Your purity will assist My power. Your

presence will keep Satan away... and Your Son, Mother,
will feel stronger knowing that You are near Him. You will
come, will you not, My sweet Mother?'
'Jesus! Dear Son! I have a feeling that You are not
happy... What is the matter, Creature of My heart? Was
the world hostile to You? No? It is a relief to believe it...
but... Oh! Yes. I will come. Wherever You wish, as and
when You wish. Even now, in this blazing sunshine, or by
night, in cold or wet weather. You want Me? Here I am.'
'No. Not now. But one day... How sweet is our home. And
Your caresses! Let Me sleep thus, with My head on Your
knees. I am so tired! I am still Your little Son... '
And Jesus really falls asleep, tired and exhausted, sitting
on the mat, His head on the lap of His Mother, Who
happily caresses His hair.

www.ingramcontent.com/pod-product-compliance
Lightning Source LLC
Chambersburg PA
CBHW060032050426
42448CB00012B/2973